John Heath-Stubbs was born in London in 1918 but spent his early years in Hampshire. At Oxford he read English and his poems were included in *Eight Oxford Poets,* edited by Sidney Keyes and Michael Meyer. After leaving Oxford he worked for a time as a schoolmaster and a publisher's hack. He has been Gregory Fellow in Poetry at the University of Leeds (1952-5), visiting Professor of English at the University of Alexandria (1955-8), and visiting Professor of English at the University of Michigan (1960-61). He now lectures in English literature at the College of St Mark and St John, Chelsea. His publications include several volumes of verse, plays, translations and criticism.

F. T. Prince says: 'Perhaps in reaction against early travels from South Africa, to Europe and the United States, and the Middle East during the war, I have lived in the same English town for the last twenty-five years. A poet does not need to live a special kind of life. In my experience an ordinary life, with marriage, children, friends, and work, is special enough. There is no difficulty in being both a scholar and a poet, except that you have to work twice as hard as other people.' F. T. Prince has been Professor of English at Southampton University since 1957.

Stephen Spender, the poet and critic, has been Professor of English at University College, London, since 1970. He went to University College School and University College, Oxford. He has edited two of the most prominent literary periodicals of the century, *Horizon* and *Encounter*. His first book of poems appeared in 1936; since then he has written an autobiography, a travel book, short stories, critical essays and six further volumes of verse.

D1513918

Penguin Modern Poets

— 20 —

JOHN HEATH-STUBBS
F. T. PRINCE
STEPHEN SPENDER

Penguin Books

Penguin Books Ltd, Harmondsworth, Middlesex, England
Penguin Books Inc., 7110 Ambassador Road, Baltimore, Maryland 21207, U.S.A.
Penguin Books Australia Ltd, Ringwood, Victoria, Australia

—

This selection first published 1972
Copyright © Penguin Books Ltd, 1971

—

Made and printed in Great Britain by
C. Nicholls & Company Ltd
Set in Monotype Garamond

This book is sold subject to the condition
that it shall not, by way of trade or otherwise,
be lent, re-sold, hired out, or otherwise circulated
without the publisher's prior consent in any form of
binding or cover other than that in which it is
published and without a similar condition
including this condition being imposed
on the subsequent purchaser

Contents

CONTENTS

Acknowledgements

For the poems by John Heath-Stubbs from *Selected Poems*, 1965, grateful acknowledgement is made to Oxford University Press, and for unpublished poems to the author.

For the poems by F. T. Prince from *The Doors of Stone*, 1963, originally published by Rupert Hart-Davis, grateful acknowledgement is made to the author; for the extracts from *Memoirs in Oxford*, 1970, grateful acknowledgement is made to Fulcrum Press.

For the poems by Stephen Spender from *Collected Poems 1928–1953*, 1955, and *The Generous Days*, 1971, grateful acknowledgement is made to Faber & Faber and the author.

JOHN HEATH-STUBBS

Leporello

Do you see that old man over there? – He was once a
    gentleman's gentleman;
His skull is bald and wrinkled like a leathery snake's egg;
His forehead is not high, but his eyes, though horny, are
    cunning,
Like an old jackdaw's beginning to moult a few grey
    feathers;
His nose is sharp like a weasel's, and his lips always a little
    smiling,
His narrow shoulders crouched forward, hinting a half-
    finished bow.
Did you notice how beautifully white and smooth and soft
    his hands were?
His coat is dowdy as the dusty shards of a house-haunting
    beetle,
His cuffs and collar not quite white, like the foam on a
    fouled mill-race.
But Fear flickers over his face – now settling like a fly
On his sunken cheeks, now haunting his blurred eyes;
And his pale mouth is always ready to fall open and gasp
    and shriek...
    Night after night he's here, in all weathers,
Drinking. They say his wife is a shrew and holds her head
    high
For all that once.... Night after night, under the yellow
    lantern-light,
Always the same old chair in the corner, night after night.
    But he likes to talk to a stranger – it makes a nice change.
Why don't you buy him a drink and get him talking?
    He can remember his master well – those were the days! –
Feast days, Carnival days – fans and flowers and bright silk
    shawls

Tossing like a poppy-patched cornfield the wind dishevels,
And then milky moonlight flowing over close-kept court-
    yards;
And while his master climbed the balcony, he would keep
    watch,
Whistle and rub his hands and gaze at the stars –
His co-panders, or there were mandolins murmuring
Lies under windows that winked and slyly slid open;
Or the hand's clutch and half-humorous gasp of the
    escapade,
And after a doubling hare's turn, choking laughter at fooled
    footsteps
Trotting away down wrong turnings; or when cornered,
The sardonic, simple, decided flash of a sword – his master's
    sword.
   And he can remember that night when he stood on the
    terrace
Sunning himself in black beams of vicarious sin,
While the waltz whispered within;
And three unaccountable late-comers came,
And gave no name –
(But she in the blue brocade is Anna:
And she has forged her outraged chastity into a blade
Of thin sharp ice-coloured steel; her hair is brown
And her eyebrows arched and black like two leaping salmon
Seen against the sun-flecked foam of a weir down-rushing;
And like a slim white hound unleashed she snuffs for the
    blood
Of a father's killer. And not far away is Elvira:
She wears silver and black and is heavily veiled
And has laid a huge jewelled crucifix over her hungry heart
In vain; for she is like an old frosty-feathered gyrfalcon,
With chrysolite eyes, mewed-up now, whose inactive perch
Frets her hooked feet; who cannot bear to gaze out

At the blue sky-paths slashed by young curving wings;
Her heart is a ruined tower from which snake-ivy
Creeps, fit to drag down an oak and smother him in dark
    green leaves.)
But the windows were all golden-spotted with candles,
Shadowed by dancing shapes; till above the silken strings
Flute and violin had trailed across the evening – a cry:
Zerlina, like a wounded hare tangled in that black net.

*

It is very quiet in the graveyard – a strange place to be
    waiting for him;
The moonlight hints queer perjuries – for all the Dead
Are tucked up snug in mud; we have heaped vast lumps of
    masonry
Over their head and their feet, fenced them round with
    crosses
And stones scrawled over with white lies; we have given
    them flowers
Against the stench, and stopped their nostrils with mud;
We have lighted candles for hollow sockets; they will not
    trouble us;
They cannot see to climb the slippery stairs of their vault;
They are blind spectators who have long dropped out of
    the game –
But what if they didn't play fair? What if cold stone
Should speak, and offer unwanted advice? What if quite
    suddenly
This polished transparently reasonable world were shattered?
When the soft curtain of the night is ripped up by the bray
    of trombones,
And a dumb stone abstraction can speak, and the madman
    invites it to supper –

That is no laughing matter. If you are young and well-born
And have no heart, it seems you can go home and laugh,
Drink wine and do yourself well; but he, Leporello,
A poor man, sir, always attentive to business, no great
  scholar,
Had never thought of these things, didn't know how to
  deal with the dead gentleman,
Or Hell stretching out a flaming hungry arm
To snatch the ripe fruit of sin from the lighted banqueting
  hall.

*

So that is why he has always a startled look, that old man;
For he feels he is being watched by dead eyes from behind
  the curtains,
And is still expecting a knock at the door, and the stone
  foot's tramp on the stairs.

Mozart

Mozart walking in the garden,
Tormented beside cool waters,
Remembered the empty-headed girl,
And the surly porters,

The singing-bird in the snuff-box,
And the clown's comic nose,
And scattered the thin blue petals
Of a steel rose.

For the Nativity

Shepherds, I sing you, this winter's night
Our Hope new-planted, the womb'd, the buried Seed:
For a strange Star has fallen, to blossom from a tomb,
And infinite Godhead circumscribed, hangs helpless at the
    breast.

Now the cold airs are musical, and all the ways of the sky
Vivid with moving fires, above the hills where tread
The feet – how beautiful! – of them that publish peace.

The sacrifice, which is not made for them,
The angels comprehend, and bend to earth
Their worshipping way. Material kind Earth
Gives Him a Mother's breast, and needful food.

A Love, shepherds, most poor,
And yet most royal, kings,
Begins this winter's night;
But oh, cast forth, and with no proper place,
Out in the cold He lies!

JOHN HEATH-STUBBS

The Divided Ways

(*In memory of Sidney Keyes*)

He has gone down into the dark cellar
To talk with the bright-faced Spirit with silver hair;
But I shall never know what word was spoken there.

*

My friend is out of earshot. Our ways divided
Before we even knew we had missed each other.
For he advanced
Into a stony wilderness of the heart,
Under a hostile and a red-clawed sun;
All that dry day, until the darkness fell,
I heard him going, and shouting among the canyons.
But I, struck backward from the eastern gate,
Had turned aside, obscure,
Beneath the unfriendly silence of the moon,
My long white fingers on a small carved lute.
There was a forest, and faces known in childhood
Rose unexpected from the mirrored pools;
The trees had hands to clutch my velvet shoulders,
And birds of fever sang among the branches;
Till the dark vine-boughs, breaking as I seized them,
And dripping blood, cried out with my own voice:
'I also have known thirst, and the wanderer's terror!...'

But I had lost my friend and the mountain paths;
And if there might have been another meeting –
The new sun rising in a different sky,
Having repaired his light in the streams of Ocean,
And the moon, white and maternal, going down

Over the virgin hills – it is too late
Ever to find it now.

And though it was in May that the reptile guns
And breeze-fly bullets took my friend away,
It is no time to forge a delicate idyll
Of the young shepherd, stricken, prone among
The flowers of spring, heavy with morning dew,
And emblematic blood of dying gods;
Or that head pillowed on a wave's white fleece,
Softly drowning in a Celtic sea.
This was more harsh and meaningless than winter.

But now, at last, I dare avow my terror
Of the pale vampire by the cooling grate;
The enemy face that doubled every loved one;
My secret fear of him and his cold heroes;
The meaning of the dream
Which was so fraught with trouble for us both;
And how through this long autumn
(Sick and tempestuous with another sorrow)
His spirit, vexed, fluttered among my thoughts,
A bird returning to the darkened window –
The hard-eyed albatross with scissor bill.
And I would ask his pardon for this weakness.

But he is gone where no hallooing voice
Nor beckoning hand can ever call him back;
And what is ours of him
Must speak impartially for all the world;
There is no personal word remains for me,
And I pretend to find no meaning here.
Though I might guess that other Singer's wisdom
Who saw in Death a dark immaculate flower,

And tenderness in every falling autumn,
This abstract music will not bring again
My friend to his warm room:
Inscrutable the darkness covers him.

Horace to Lydia

(Odes I, xxv)

Of late it's not so often one can hear
Your shutters rattling, nor young wenchers jar
Your slumbers; the accommodating door
                        Hugs close its threshold,

Whose hinges once so easily found occasion;
This serenade grows less and less in fashion:
'Can you, while I am dying out here of passion,
                        Lie sleeping, Lydia?'

You too, a broken-down hag in some dark alley,
Shall weep the insults of your faithless cully,
When, between moons, comes like a drunken bully,
                        The North Wind raging;

While a fierce lust, with unappeasable fires,
Such as in rutting time drives mad the mares,
Sends through your ulcerated guts its flares,
                        And its frustration;

Because young men prefer the fresh green shoot,
The ivy and the myrtle when they're sweet,
And fling the dry leaves that with winter wilt
                        Down the cold river.

Ibycus

When the city cast out the best
   In a clamour of indecision,
I had no breath to waste
   Cobbling up their division;
I unhooked the lyre from its peg,
   Turned ship to the Samian shore.
I call no one to witness
   But the clanging birds of the air.

The quince-tree garden is shattered,
   The vine-shoots fail in Spring;
Down from the Thracian mountains,
   On fire with the lightning,
Love comes, like a blackguard wind.
   Love was betrayal and fear.
I call no one to witness
   But the clanging birds of the air.

The open-handed I praise,
   Great-souled Polycrates,
Pride of whose tinted galleons
   Ruled the Ionian seas.
Treachery took him – nailed
   For the crows to peck him bare.
I call no one to witness
   But the clanging birds of the air.

Twilight: a narrow place:
   Armed men blocking the road.
Gold glisters on my finger.
   In chevron high overhead
The southward-journeying cranes –

What Erinnyes are here?
I call no one to witness
But the clanging birds of the air.

Address Not Known

So you are gone, and are proved bad change, as we had
   always known,
And I am left lonely in London the metropolitan city,
Perhaps to twist this incident into a durable poem –
The lesson of those who give their love to phenomenal
   beauty.

I am coming to think now that all I have loved were
   shadows
Strayed up from a dead world, through a gap in a raped
   tomb,
Or where the narcissus battens in mythological meadows:
Your face was painted on the coffin-lid from Fayoum.

Is this my pain that is speaking? The pain was not long
   protracted:
I make a statement, forgive the betrayal, the meanness, the
   theft.
Human, I cannot suppose you had planned all that was
   enacted:
Fortitude must be procured to encounter the hollowness
   left.

The sun will not haver in its course for the lack of you,
Nor the flowers fail in colour, nor the bird stint in its song.
Only the heart that wanted somehow to have opened up
Finds the frost in the day's air, and the nights which appear
   too long.

Obstinate in Non-Attendance

Obstinate in non-attendance I cannot but think kindly
Of the county of Hampshire, my nurse; she is sluttish but
   not uncomely:
Sociable in London my heart is a parched forest
And my skull a stone tower where the songs not easily nest.

But she who fostered my first cares and my loneliness,
Indifferent yet received them with a certain homeliness:
My tears hardly augment the griefs that in Thames must
   run,
But could add a saltness to the Stour's, or the Avon's, urn.

The Celt rants in my blood; but it is of Winchester
The Saxon monarchs who lift up a golden sceptre
To rule in all my dreams with a plain civility,
Though my ancestors rowed Edgar the Peaceable on the
   Dee.

Or striving in my verse to acclimatize the Italian myrtle
And the Greek cyclamen, I sometimes feel it is futile:
The yellow gorse the coltsfoot and the rest-harrow
Are nourished by the clay and sand that fed my earliest
   sorrow.

JOHN HEATH-STUBBS

Canticle of the Sun

Dancing on Easter Morning

I am the great Sun. This hour begins
My dancing day – pirouetting in a whirl of white light
In my wide orchestral sky, a red ball bouncing
Across the eternal hills;
For now my Lord is restored: with the rising dew
He carries his own up to his glittering kingdom –
Benedicite, benedicite, benedicite omnia opera.

Look, I am one of the morning stars, shouting for joy –
And not the least honoured among those shining brothers,
O my planetary children – now that my dark daughter,
The prodigal Earth, is made an honest woman of;
Out of her gapped womb, her black and grimy tomb,
Breaks forth the Crowned, victory in his pierced hands –
Benedicite, benedicite benedicite, omnia opera.

You too, my lovers – little lark with trembling feathers,
Sing your small heart out in my streaming rays;
And you, grave narrow-browed eagle, straining your eyes
Against my wound – foretell
These fiery dales and flame-anemoned meadows
Shall be a haunt for shy contemplative spirits –
Benedicite, benedicite, benedicite omnia opera.

And now with joy I run my recurring race;
And though again I shall have to hide my face
With a hand of cloud out of the heart of schism,
Yet the time is sure when I once more shall be
A burning giant in his marriage-chamber,
A bright gold cherub, as I came from my Father's halls –
Benedicite, benedicite, benedicite omnia opera.

The Lady's Complaint

I speak of that lady I heard last night,
  Maudlin over her gin and water,
In a sloppy bar with a fulvous light
  And an air that was smeared with smoke and laughter:
  How youth decamps and cold age comes after,
In fifty years she had found it true –
  She sighed for the damage that time had brought her:
'Oh, after death there's a judgement due.

'What once was as sleek as a seal's pelt,
  My shapeless body has fallen from grace;
My soul and my shoes are worn down to the welt,
  And no cosmetic can mask my face,
  As under talcum and oxide you trace
How the bones stick out, and the ghost peeps through –
  A wanderer, I, in Wraith-bone Place,
And after death there's a judgement due.

'My roundabout horses have cantered away,
  The gilded and garrulous seasons are flown;
What echo is left of the rag-time bray
  Of the tenor sax and the susaphone?
  But I was frightened to sleep alone
(As now I must do, as now I must do)
  And a chittering bat-voice pipes "Atone,
For after death there's a judgement due."

'Green apples I bit when I was green,
  My teeth are on edge at the maggoty core;
Life is inclement, obscure, obscene;
  Nothing's amusing – not any more;
  But love's abrasions have left me sore –

To hairy Harry and half-mast Hugh
   I gave the love I was starving for,
And after death there's a judgement due.

'Potentate, swirling in stark cold air
   The corn from the husks – I offer to you
My terror-struck and incredulous prayer,
   For after death there's a judgement due.'

Girl with Marionettes

(LEEDS CITY VARIETIES)

To John Betjeman

They hold their own, not the wire-puller's laws,
As each its wicked, sensual life assumes;
The prancing skeleton gained our applause.

That invocation gave our laughter pause:
These manikins our merriment exhumes –
They hold their own, not the wire-puller's laws.

The grave-faced girl, thus, cautiously withdraws
Them from their box, like mummies from old tombs –
The prancing skeleton gained our applause.

The erotic nautch-doll, draped in tinselled gauze,
Twitches her stiff limbs to Ketélby's neumes;
They hold their own, not the wire-puller's laws.

And vanishing at last, as with no cause –
Magnesium flash, and puff of bluish fumes –
The prancing skeleton gained our applause.

To abolish chaos, and restore guffaws,
Three teddy-bears in hand, she now presumes;
They hold their own, not the wire-puller's laws –
The prancing skeleton gained our applause.

Epitaph for Thaïs

Traveller, under this stone lies all that remains – of our
    sister,
  Arete, servant of Christ; alkaline sands of Natroun
Hold here a wonder, those limbs which once lent their
        contours to Thaïs
  (God has forgiven her sins – scarlet, now whiter than
        snow).
Ask not how many young men their fortunes let slip, and
        careers,
  Chancing one night on her couch (and it was worth it,
        they said);
Neo-Platonic sages failed to show up at their lectures –
  Dream of the touch of her lips, metaphysics go hang!
Praising one of her nipples, there was a poet composed an
  Epic in twenty-two books (no one peruses it now).
Alexandria's side-streets are always full of such rumours
  (Keep to the lives of the Saints, these are the gossip of
        Heaven).
All is altered now; she who was bound to the shameless
  Demon the heathen revere, Aphrodite the Rose,
Now is made free of the golden-causewayed city of Zion
  (Love that accomplishes all, glory be given to Thee).
Athanäel our brother with his rough rhetoric tamed this
  Lamb that so widely had strayed, coaxing it back to the
        fold.

Athanäel has left us; dying, they say in despair – he
  Could find no quiet nor rest, such are the snares of the
        Fiend –
So distracted his prayers the rose-tinctured body of Thaïs
  Satan into his den clawed that apostatized soul.

Did you suppose, O you who pass by, this hetaira
   Yielded herself to a god, not exacting her price?
What more costly a gem could Heaven itself afford than,
   Dear-bought and bright, a soul, predestined, to her fee?

The Cave of the Nymphs

Hushed, haunted the cave – a gathering point
For time and eternity. One entrance
For men, subject to death,
One, open to the sky,
For the Undying. In this place,
Where the quiet nymphs weave purple cloth,
And hive the learnèd bees – archetypes,
Images, symbols.

But Ulysses,
Ulysses of the many stratagems,
Was unaware of this. He shook himself (grandson
of Autolycus, the wolf-man) suddenly awake
Like a great canine. He rubbed the salt from his eyes,
Dismissing the images of night and journeying:
The snatching horror, the sucking whirlpool,
Canticle of the death-birds,
Possessive and beast-attended
Goddesses, the geometrical gardens.
He knew where he was. The landscape
Was not the deceptive pastoral simplicity
Of the cannibals' island, and not
The hothouse vegetation of Lotos-land,
Nor spruce and silver-birch
Of the Laestrygones' fjord. It was limestone;
It was tamarisks; it was olives
And vine-stocks gnawed by goats.
It was Ithaca at last. And was dangerous.

Therefore, out in the sunlight,
Meeting a shepherd-boy,
He started once more to lie –

It was almost routine with him now –
Improvising a cover-story. But with so much blague,
And such a ready tongue,
He began to enjoy it. And that other,
Knowing it would all come out,
Could not refrain from revealing herself –
The goddess who was on his side –
And chaffed him too. So they stood there,
The man and the Immortal, like a pair of friends
Who understand each other
Too well to talk much.

And as he turned to go
She still smiled after him. But if
The perdurable and inviolate heart
Of immortal Wisdom might grieve, it ached then
For what it could never know:
For not to know death is to know nothing
Of the wonder of deliverance; and to be free
Of the wide aether, and the white peaks of Olympos,
And all the bounds of the world and the backward-flowing
    Ocean,
Is never to know and love
One patch of earth as home.

                    But Ulysses,
Ulysses who had made a good journey,
Was unaware of this. He had gone to look for
A wife he had not met
For twenty years, and a son
Who must now be a stranger to him.
For he had come home;
Which is the whole point of the story.

Not Being Oedipus

Not being Oedipus he did not question the Sphinx
Nor allow it to question him. He thought it expedient
To make friends and try to influence it.
In this he entirely succeeded,

And continued his journey to Thebes. The abominable
    thing
Now tame as a kitten (though he was not unaware
That its destructive claws were merely sheathed)
Lolloped along beside him –

To the consternation of the Reception Committee.
It posed a nice problem: he had certainly overcome
But not destroyed the creature – was he or was he not
Entitled to the hand of the Princess

Dowager Jocasta? Not being Oedipus
He saw it as a problem too. For frankly he was not
By natural instinct at all attracted to her.
The question was soon solved –

Solved itself, you might say; for while they argued
The hungry Sphinx, which had not been fed all day,
Sneaked off unobserved, penetrated the royal apartments,
And softly consumed the lady.

So he ascended the important throne of Cadmus,
Beginning a distinguished and uneventful reign.
Celibate, he had nothing to fear from ambitious sons;
Although he was lonely at nights,

With only the Sphinx, curled up upon his eiderdown.
Its body exuded a sort of unearthly warmth

(Though in fact cold-blooded) but its capacity
For affection was strictly limited.

Granted, after his death it was inconsolable,
And froze into its own stone effigy
Upon his tomb. But this was self-love, really –
It felt it had failed in its mission.

While Thebes, by common consent of the people, adopted
His extremely liberal and reasonable constitution,
Which should have enshrined his name – but not being
    Oedipus,
It vanished from history, as from legend.

Plato and the Waters of the Flood

In one of the remoter parts of Asia Minor, near what was once the southern boundary of the Phrygians, there is a warm spring flanked by a Hittite monument, and known to the Turks as Plato's Spring. The reason for the name is that it was at this spot, according to Arab legend, that Plato succeeded in stopping the Flood by making the waters run underground. (W. K. C. GUTHRIE, *Orpheus and Greek Religion*).

When on Armenian Ararat
  Or Parnassus ridge
Scrunched the overloaded keel,
  Pelican, ostrich,
Toad, rabbit, and pangolin –
  All the beasts of the field –
Scrambled out to possess once more
  Their cleansed and desolate world,
      Plato, by that fountain,
        Spoke to the swirling deep:
      'Retire, you waters of Chaos,
        Flow retrograde, and sleep;
      Above the swift revolving heavens
        Rule the intelligible,
      Chaste and undecaying ideas;
        Brackish waters, fall!'

Plato, in the academic grove,
  Among the nightingales,
Expounded to wide-eyed ephebes
  His geometric rules;
Reared a republic in the mind
  Where only noble lies

Reign; he expelled the poets
  (With courtesy, with praise).

Loaded with useless garlands,
  Down to that fountain
The exiled poets proceeded:
  'When will you rise again,
Ten-horned, seven-headed seraphim,
  Out of your abyss,
Against the beautiful Republic –
  Nor tamed by Plato's kiss?'

JOHN HEATH-STUBBS

Titus and Berenice*

'Turn to me in the darkness,
    Asia with your cool
Gardens beyond the desert,
    Your clear, frog-haunted pool;
I seek your reassurance –
    Forget, as I would forget,
Your holy city cast down, the Temple
    That still I desecrate.'
'Buzz!' said the blue-fly in his head.

'In darkness master me,
    Rome with your seven hills,
Roads, rhetorical aqueducts,
    And ravaging eagles;
Worlds are at bitter odds, yet we
    Have our love at least –
Not expedient to the Senate,
    Abominable to the priest.'
'Buzz!' said the blue-fly in his head.

Titus the clement Emperor
    And she of Herod's house
Slobbered and clawed each other
    Like creatures of the stews;
Lay together, then lay apart
    And knew they had not subdued –
She the insect in his brain,
    Nor he her angry God.

*NOTE: According to a Jewish tradition Titus was afflicted with an
insect in his brain as a punishment for his destruction of the temple.

Ars Poetica

I

One thing *imprimis* I would have you remember:
Your poetry is no good
Unless it move the heart. And the human heart,
The heart which you must move,
Is corrupt, depraved, and desperately wicked

Milton denoted poetry
'Simple, sensuous and passionate'.
But who has said, my dear,
Human sensuality and human passion
Were ever simple matters?

But poetry is not 'emotional truth'.
The emotions have much less to do with the business
Than is commonly supposed. No more than the intellect.
The intellect shapes, the emotions feed the poem,
Whose roots are in the senses, whose flower is imagination.

Call it then: 'A humane science'
(Like all science concerned
With a world that really exists) – but humane:
Beatrice could request, not command Virgil –
She among the blessed, and he in Limbo –
He can take you as far as the Earthly Paradise
But no further than that.

In Limbo also is the Master of them that know:
But he is a Master. Therefore respect critics,
Especially the uncomfortable ones.

But there is no field of any activity
In which the parable of the wheat and the tares
Is more applicable.

The poem does not propound
Your or anyone else's opinions,
However admirable, however fascinating;
With luck it may touch the skirts
Of universal Wisdom.

And much the same goes for the passions:
The oaf in love *may* be a poet
Or bumpkin tongue-tied still;
A poet in love may be no less oafish.
And so in eloquence remember
All things exist in Love.

I mentioned just now luck – our Lady Fortune
('Bright-haired daughter of Chaos' I once called her)
She also is an exalted goddess,
Germane to the Muse. Therefore revere her.

2

A poem is built out of words;
And words are not your property.
They are common counters, involved
In private chaffering, and international transactions;
They have been tossed into the caps of beggars, and
    plonked
On the reception-desks of brothels.

In your case they are the English language:
Not the Greek flute, nor the Roman trumpet,
Nor the Welsh harp, nor the Spanish guitar,

Nor the French clavecin,
But a sound bourgeois piano
Capable of something of each.

You have got to make language say
What it has not said before;
Otherwise why bother – after a millennium,
(And a bit more) of English poetry – and you a wren
Rising from the eagle's back?
Work against language. It is your enemy.
Engage in a bout with it.
But like a Japanese wrestler
You will overcome by not resisting.

3

The words come to you from the commercial districts:
From the shop-bench, and from working in the fields;
But contrary to much of the practice of the age
There is something to be said for politely requesting them
To wipe the mud off their boots
Before they tread on your carpet
(Supposing you own one).

And if they should emerge from the reading-room
Tactfully suggest they remove the cheese-parings,
Dead flies and biscuit-crumbs from among their whiskers.

I have no personal objection
If you want to put on singing robes:
At a ritual you don't wear work-a-day clothes.
But the surplice and chasuble, or the Geneva gown
Are nothing more than the Sunday best
Of a Byzantine gentleman, or a Renaissance scholar;

And any clergyman, I suppose, would look pretty silly
If he walked down the street in them.

So under existing social conditions
You had better think over this matter of your costume
With a certain perspicacity.

4

A poem is like an iceberg:
Seven-tenths under water
(And what is below the surface –
This may at first have seemed
To you the most important.)
Like an iceberg – cold, hard,
Jagged and chaste, glittering
With prismatic colours, as it drifts
On unpredictable deep-sea tides. Against it also
The titanic folly of the age
May shatter itself as it goes through its joyless night.

5

'Patience and perseverance
Made a bishop in his reverence.'
The proverb ought to have added
'And the charisma of the Holy Ghost.'

Mutatis mutandis
(And it is very much *mutandis*)
This likewise is relevant.

So through patience, perseverance, luck and that sort of
    thing
(I can only wish you luck)

You may arrive at an actual poem –
An interjected remark
At a party which has been going on
For quite a time (and will, we trust, continue);
A party at which you are not
A specially favoured guest
And which you will have to leave before it is over.

Let us hope the others will occasionally recall it.

But to you it will seem a little world.
You will look at your creation and see that it is good.
In this you will be mistaken:
You are not, after all, God.

from *A Little Bestiary*

THE HARE

Would rather run up-hill than down-hill;
Would rather look backwards than forwards;
Escapes by going the long way round,
Or by lying still.

Mad? A wild lover,
And a bouncing prize-fighter;
But, a careful mother,
In tussocks of couch-grass
Abandons her leverets.

Wounded, captured, screams
Horribly, like a child;
Is eaten half-putrid, boiled
In its own dark blood;

And is sacred to the Moon,
A type of innocent sacrifice.

Song for St Valentine's Day

Urbane bishop, Valentine,
    Sexually ensnarling
Tom with Thomasina tit,
    Starling with his darling,
Cob swan with pen swan,
    Dove with truest turtle,
Ducks with drakes, and ruffs with reeves,
    Under Venus' myrtle:

On plastic macs beside tilled fields
    Copulating couples
Do the essentially innocent act –
    Till they bit those apples,
Down in Eden's seminal garden,
    Poor Adam, silly Eve,
Created into a world of matter
    Where scaly worms deceive.

Within your airy diocese
    Feathered reptiles flutter –
Twitter and caw, and bill and coo
    What they cannot utter:
A man and a woman upon a bed
    Gasp and groan and sigh
'Unto us a child is given,
    But we two must die.'

Exalted martyr, Valentine,
    Teach me this pervigilium
Why the rape of Helen was worth
    The burning down of Ilium;
Of Love, continually crucified;

Eternally throned above,
Comprehending within itself
All things. Including love.

When Sappho Loved

When Sappho loved a gondolier
  Tongues on Lesbos clacked apace:
Unhappily he had no ear
    For stanzas of Aeolian grace;
      Her lover's leap into the deep
        Fishily-tanged Tyrrhenian tide –
      One sickening drop – soon put a stop
        To lyric passion and to pride.

Lady Mary laughed to view
  Great Mr Pope before her kneeling:
His form seemed ill-designed to woo,
    Much less evoke an answering feeling:
      So Alexander lived to slander
        What else he tenderly had sung,
      And she confessed among the rest
        The Asp of Twickenham's forked tongue.

Dispersed about the Delphic plane
  Grasshopper-witted poets thrum –
You scurrying ants who haul the grain
    Envy them not though you be dumb:
      What's to your mind perhaps you'll find
        At harvest's end among the sheaves
      But those who follow bright Apollo
        Likely embrace cold laurel leaves.

JOHN HEATH-STUBBS

Variation on a Theme
by George Darley

It is not beauty I desire
   And not – but not – the virtuous mind:
Marks of potential tragedy –
   These stigmatize the human kind.

And lonely in the darkness, I
   Surmise your pain, your loneliness
And stretch uneasy arms towards
   That inarticulate distress.

If sons and daughters of the gods
   Stride careless through the market-place
What can we but avert our eyes –
   Acknowledge, not demand, their grace?

Although the smooth olympian brow
   Bids Greece and Ilium beware,
More turbid tides on love's dark sea
   Involve us with the siren's hair.

Each hard-faced doctor who expounds
   Within the rigid schools avers
That God Himself loves His elect
   Yet for no merit that is theirs.

And, fuel to the appalling creed,
   By human analogues we know
We do not love the beautiful
   But, loved, they are imputed so.

The Timeless Nightingale

A nightingale sat perched upon
    The trellis of a Samian vine
Beneath whose shade Anacreon
    Strung his slight lyre, and drank his wine;
Far in the Asian highlands then
    The corpse of great Polycrates
Was scorched by sun and stripped by rain,
    Stretched on the cross-bars of two trees;
But the nightingale's lament
    Was for dismembered Itylus:
White-haired Anacreon vainly schemed –
    How could he move Cleobulus.
    The poet took another glass.

Li Po drank his rice-spirit warm:
    Disgraced at court, he sipped alone –
No one to talk to or make love –
    Himself, his shadow, and the moon;
Above his head, migrating cranes:
    In the wild gorges monkeys howl:
Red-haired, green-eyed barbarians
    Along the utmost marches prowl;
The nightingale (or what bird else
    Chinese convention had assigned)
Fluted of jewelled gardens where
    Drunken immortals ride the wind.
    The poet took another glass.

Upon a greenish sky at dawn
    The sickle of the moon grew dim:
Hafiz still sat there on the lawn:
    A moon-browed Saki poured for him;

Advanced across the Northern hills
   Timur and his crude Turkish band,
To build their pyramids of skulls,
   And fetch the wine to Samarkand;
But the timeless nightingale
   Enamoured of the eternal rose
Cried 'Love's in the dark of the candle-flame,
   And nothing quite what we suppose!'
     The poet took another glass.

The true, the blushful Hippocrene
   Was fairish claret, if you please:
Love a bacillus in his lung,
   John Keats was on those perilous seas;
Into the mills of Lancashire
   The Luddite gangs walked stark and grim:
The bourgeois Muse was mousy-haired
   And did not only dance with him;
The nightingale inside his head
   Sang on (one voice to him and Ruth)
'You're better off when you are dead –
   Truth's Beauty then, and Beauty truth.'
     The poet took another, took another glass.

from *Artorius*

CAPRICORN

Not even on Olympus are the Immortals exempt
From the ravages of change, and the revolutions of
    chance;
The sadness of senility likewise seizes them,
Entailing its empty and impotent wisdom.
Saturn with his sceptre once swayed the universe;
And governed the earth in the Age of Gold –
The first men in scattered families followed
The herds of beasts, hunting the bison,
The mammoth and the reindeer, as they ranged, for meat.
A simple collectivity, a classless society,
Not ploughing the soil, nor in seed-time sowing.
Their craft, from the flint crudely to fashion
The tools for their tasks, and with tinted ochre,
In lightless caverns, to limn and character,
Magically, the beasts, to make them breed,
Or slide into the pit, to be pierced by spears.
The bones of their dead they daubed and bedabbled
Likewise with red, for luck and for life,
And gold – prized for its grace and its gladness,
Mysteriously life-giving, not the miser's loot.
But Jove revolted; in rebellion he wrested
The sceptre from his sire, and sent him into exile
To a western island, in the wide ocean;
There he sleeps through time, with the Titans, his
    siblings –
Grimly, the huge hundred-hander guards them.
A new age now was known on the earth:
Agriculture was invented, and astronomy also,
To mark the succession of the circling seasons,

For hoeing and sowing, and the hauling in of harvest.
In the stone circles men hallowed the sun,
And the feminine and magical mysteries of the moon.
Human blood, holy and blessing
The soil, was sacrificed, the priest-king was slaughtered
Yearly, for the plenty he yielded to the plants.
Priests also and traders, in the towns, proliferated,
Subsisting from the labour of their serfs on their land;
Silver was hoarded, and a hieratic script
Enrolled their secrets, and recorded their revenues.

The Age of Bronze awoke now in brutality:
Barbarian warriors blustered out of the wastelands,
And wars were waged with more effective weapons.
The handsome heroes exhibited their hardihood
In wild tumult, by windy Troys,
Fighting in chariots, fiercely cheered on
To plunder and pillage, by Homeric poets.

The Age of Iron, out of Asia, extended
A worse development of destruction – war
Become less human, more horrible and more hideous;
The wheel is in motion, willy-nilly we march on
To the uses of artillery, and atomic overkill.
Each technical gain entails the giving up
Of a spiritual good, of certainty and security.
This puts paid, we presume, to that specious puerility
Which professes to hail, in History, a progress.
Mutability masters us – no myth of improvement
Is the law of life; laugh it off, if you will –
Anangke is the arbitress, and enjoins us: 'Adapt!'

The Saturnalia was celebrated at the Winter Solstice

In remembrance, by the Romans, of the reign of Saturn:
By ritualized ribaldry, and licensed riot –
The posts are decked, the porticoes and the doorways,
With gaiety of greenery, and gifts exchanged;
The slaves sit down and are served by their masters,
Reconstructing a far-off and irrecoverable freedom
Nostalgically lost in the long-ago of legend,
When the world was governed by wiser gods.
But at this season of mid-winter mirth, the Saviour,
Christ, was born in the cavern at Bethlehem,
To oust from Olympus the etiolated eidola;
Jove and his fellows fell under the judgement
Of old age also, and entered that emptiness
Where man's lost dreams dwindle in darkness.
The stable, for once, was the centre of the world;
Not the dialectical dragons, but the dumb ox
And the ass in humility, hung their heads
By a manger of straw, where Mary the Mother
Looked at her Love and hushed Him with a lullaby.
From the Solstice of Capricorn the Cross stems up,
The ends of the transom transfixing the equinoxes,
The summit at Cancer – Christ in the circle
Of the stars of fatality, to ensure our freedom,
Slain for our salvation, in the celestial wheel,
From the foundation of the world; He was found worthy.

At this Feast it is the kindly custom of Christians
To honour in each other the Divine Image
By the giving of gifts; as with incense and gold,
And with myrrh, the Magi from the marches of the world
Were beckoned to Bethlehem by a bright comet.
Feasting and frolic and jollity are found here –
Not the mirth of Saturn's mythical magisterium,
But the felt prescience of a possible freedom

Eschatologically offered at the end of the ages,
Whose shoots are burgeoning, and begin now to show.

But the Prince of Darkness delights to pervert this:
The affluent honour Gluttony and Avarice,
In spewing drunkenness and a spending spree,
Guzzling their guts and giving for advantage,
Disdaining the Lazaruses who languish at their doors.
In Gehenna these gourmets will get their reward –
Trussed up and transformed into battery turkeys,
With sprigs of holly stuck in their holes;
In the form of a foolish and florid Santa Claus,
With cottonwool whiskers, as a witty contrivance,
Beelzebub bastes them with their own butter.

To a Poet a Thousand Years Hence

I who am dead a thousand years
And wrote this crabbed post-classic screed
Transmit it to you – though with doubts
That you possess the skill to read,

Who, with your pink, mutated eyes,
Crouched in the radioactive swamp,
Beneath a leaking shelter, scan
These lines beside a flickering lamp;

Or in some plastic paradise
Of pointless gadgets, if you dwell,
And finding all your wants supplied
Do not suspect it may be Hell.

But does our art of words survive –
Do bards within that swamp rehearse
Tales of the twentieth century,
Nostalgic, in rude epic verse?

Or do computers churn it out –
In lieu of songs of War and Love,
Neat slogans by the State endorsed
And prayers to *them*, who sit above?

How shall we conquer? – all our pride
Fades like a summer sunset's glow:
Who will read me when I am gone –
For who reads Elroy Flecker now?

Unless, dear poet, you were born,
Like me, a deal behind your time,
There is no reason you should read,
And much less understand, this rhyme.

Celebration for a Birth

(S. J. W., born 23 December 1967)

Indifferent weather
She has brought with her
Sour sleet, together
    With a North-East wind;
While influenza,
Like a devil's cadenza,
And the cattle-murrains, are
Hurled through the land.

I summon with reason
All saints of the season
On this occasion,
    For graces to sue:
St Stephen I inveigle,
And St John the Evangel
With his wide-winged eagle,
    And the Innocents too;

Sylvester, take heed,
Pious Lucian, at need,
To wish her God-speed
    On her pilgrimage here,
And the Three Kings, whose bones
Lie shrined in the stones
Of Augustan Cologne's
    Cathedral floor.

As sisters fatal,
Stand by the cradle,
Good gifts to ladle,

The nymphs of the streams;
For I will have brought here
The lost Bayswater,
With Westbourne, the daughter
    Of paternal Thames.

They are not seen now,
But in sewers obscene, are
Thralls to Cloacina
    With her garland of mud;
But I will release them,
And of durance ease them,
If it will please them
    To perform this good.

Child, there's no need you
At all should pay heed to
Those who would mislead you,
    If ever they can:
The troubled heads of Greece –
Even great Sophocles,
With 'Not to be born is' (if you please!)
    '*The best for man.*'

Pagan delusion
And Gentile abusion
Cause the confusion
    Of their careless talk;
And for this sin, lo,
With arms akimbo,
They sit down in Limbo
    In eternal sulk.

For birth is a blessing,
Though there's no guessing

To what sad issues
    Our life may go;
And when Time shall show it,
And you, too, know it,
Say that a poet
    Told you so.

Woodstock

Rose of the world, corrupted rose –
About and about the maze path goes:

A thread of silk is caught in his spur,
A spider's clue for Eleanor –

Uprooted rose of Aquitaine
(The poets are singing to England's queen).

The dagger, the green juice in the bowl,
The toads are sucking the breasts of my soul.

And up in arms, they are marching on –
Sodomite Richard and lackland John.

At Trinity-tide the rose is in bloom
For the priest who reigns from his crusted tomb.

And Ireland is up in arms, and curses
The English laws and the English verses.

Plantagenet turns his face to the wall:
'But where is the fairest rose of all?'

A Formality

In Memoriam T.S.E.

Poetry is a formality: a continual greeting and
    leave-taking
For all that we encounter between
A darkness and a darkness. Hail and farewell
To the seven-braided spectrum. At dawn, at sunset;
And each particular thing we learn to love
We must learn to do without. Celebrate this;
Poetry is a formality.

Poetry is a formality: with words we clothe
The naked abstract thought, shivering in its shame –
Only with leaves, only with coats of skin? We can do
    more –
Go brave through the infected winter
Of our condition. Carnival.
Mask yourself, then. Poetry
Is a formality.

Poetry is a formality: to each
His way of speaking. I would emulate rather those
Who countered despair with elegance, emptiness with a
    grace.
And one there is now to be valedicted
With requiem. Poetry also? Also poetry is
A formality.

Hornbills in Northern Nigeria

(*To Hilary Fry*)

As if their great bone-spongey beaks were too heavy,
A party of Grey Hornbills flops overhead
Through the hot, humid air. These are on migration –
('Well, you tell me where,' the zoologist said) –

They emit high, whining, almost gull-like cries,
Seeming, someone remarks, as if they were
    mass-produced
Off the production-line of an inferior factory.
But this is not apt. Has it not been deduced

The grotesque Hornbill stems from an ancient race
By the fossil testimony of a small, stony word,
Petrified bone-fragment in alluvial clay?
Look again, you witness a prehistoric bird;

On miocene and pliocene landscapes has gazed
The cold, saurian, humanly eyelashed eye,
Which looks out now over the airfield,
Where forms of camels – not incongruous – stray.

And ceremonial trumpets welcome the guest who comes
By Comet or Viscount, out of the modern century;
The place is not distant from the medieval walls,
Nor the satellite-tracking station (Project Mercury).

Here unashamed, anthropomorphic gods send rain;
And dawn, like history, flames a violent birth,
Out of a night with crickets and toads articulate,
For black bodies pushing ground-nuts into the red earth.

Homage to J. S. Bach

It is good just to think about Johann Sebastian
Bach, grinding away like the mills of God,
Producing masterpieces, and legitimate children –
Twenty-one in all – and earning his bread

Instructing choirboys to sing their *ut re mi*,
Provincial and obscure. When Fame's trumpets told
Of Handel displaying magnificent wings of melody,
Setting the waters of Thames on fire with gold,

Old Bach's music did not seem to the point:
He groped in the Gothic vaults of polyphony,
Labouring pedantic miracles of counterpoint.
They did not know that the order of eternity

Transfiguring the order of the Age of Reason,
The timeless accents of super-celestial harmonies,
Filtered into time through that stupendous brain.
It was the dancing angels in their hierarchies,

Teaching at the heart of Reason that Passion existed,
And at the heart of Passion a Crucifixion,
Or when the great waves of his *Sanctus* lifted
The blind art of music into a blinding vision.

Volund

(On first looking into Auden's and Taylor's *Edda*)

I had read the tale before, and thought it
A catalogue of mythological horrors. But now I read it
    again
And know the significance. And I wonder
What craftsman-smith, captive or thrall,
Amid the violence of the Viking age,
In the bitterness of his heart
Devised this savage fable.

Through Murk Wood they flew, three girls,
Triple and identical, in swanfeather dress
Whistling through the bare branches, to sojourn
Nine seasons of love. Then they departed.

'We will ride to the ends of the earth,
To East and South, to seek them!' But Volund remained,
Lonely in Wolfdale, forging rings
Of red gold, waiting her return.

He counted his rings. One was missing. He dreamed
She had come back. When he next woke
He found himself in fetters; lamed,
Relegated to an island, forced to work
At trumpery trinkets.

'All shall be told, all:
The bodies of your boys
Lie under the blood-stained bellows; I have debauched
Your daughter to a drunken slut. But now I rise
On swan's wings. I am the Lord of the Elves,
Riding the cloudless air.'

(As Dionysus, also,
Over the house of Pentheus.)

So they think they can hamstring the artist, do they –
Sever his sinews, dissever him from his Muse?

His Excellency's Poetry

'His Excellency's poetry is mainly enigmatic' –
The reply of the interpreter, for the Chinese Ambassador,
To Robert Browning. The Chinese Ambassador,
Being, as the interpreter had explained,
A considerable poet in his own language,
Had expressed a desire to encounter
An English poet. Robert Browning,
A largely self-educated Nonconformist,
Was somewhat out of his depth. He had asked
Whether His Excellency's poetry
Was epic, lyric or dramatic?

In the year 1969 *et seq.*
I think of myself as an exile and an ambassador;
Confronted with a similar question, as I not infrequently
     am,
At cocktail parties and so on, I am tempted
To come back with a similar reply.

In Return for the Gift of a Pomander

(To Cathy Tither)

I am not that butcher's son
   Of Norwich, the proud Cardinal,
Detesting so the common run,
   He could not pass among them all
Without an orange stuffed with cloves
   Clutched in his white, ringed hands, to quench
The breath of those plebeian droves,
   Their stockfish, leek, and garlic stench;
Though some, who do not love me much,
   Might say I am no democrat,
And that my attitudes are such –
   We will not argue about that:
But I affirm the gift you bring
   Discreetly with my togs shall go,
The night-marauder's silken wing
   To avaunt – although, indeed, we know
There's no sublunary gear
But moth and rust corrupt it here.

The fragrance of a generous thought
Remains. And that cannot be bought.

The Blameless Aethiopians

My Muse is away dining
With the blameless Aethiopians:
When an Immortal cannot be contacted Homer says
That is where she is.

The blameless anecdotes she formerly
Retailed to me, are whispered
Into an Aethiopian's
Jewel-studded ear.

On Aethiopian mountains
The plantain-eater hoots from the plantain tree:
Has she forgotten the English missel-thrush?

She feasts on Aethiopian delicacies,
And I could only offer her
Braised neck of lamb with carrots.

I do not really blame
The Aethiopians. In love
It takes two to make a silence.

A Few Strokes on the Sand

Old men, as they grow older, grow the more garrulous,
Drivelling *temporis acti* into their beards,
Argumentative, theoretical, diffuse.

With the poet, not so. One learns
To be spare of words; to make cold thrusts
Into the frosty air that comes.

The final message – a few strokes on the sand;
A bird's footprints running to take off
Into the adverse wind.

F. T. PRINCE

An Epistle to a Patron

My lord, hearing lately of your opulence in promises and
    your house
Busy with parasites, of your hands full of favours, your
    statutes
Admirable as music, and no fear of your arms not
    prospering, I have
Considered how to serve you and breed from my talents
These few secrets which I shall make plain
To your intelligent glory. You should understand that I
    have plotted,
Being in command of all the ordinary engines
Of defence and offence, a hundred and fifteen buildings
Less others less complete: complete, some are courts of
    serene stone,
Some the civil structures of a war-like elegance as bridges,
Sewers, aqueducts and citadels of brick, with which I
    declare the fact
That your nature is to vanquish. For these I have
    acquired a knowledge
Of the habits of numbers and of various tempers, and
    skill in setting
Firm sets of pure bare members which will rise, hanging
    together
Like an argument, with beams, ties and sistering
    pilasters:
The lintels and windows with mouldings as round as a
    girl's chin; thresholds
To libraries; halls that cannot be entered without a
    sensation as of myrrh
By your vermilion officers, your sages and dancers. There
    will be chambers
Like the recovery of a sick man, your closet waiting not

Less suitably shadowed than the heart, and the coffers of
    a ceiling
To reflect your diplomatic taciturnities. You may
    commission
Hospitals, huge granaries that will smile to bear your
    filial plunders,
And stables washed with a silver lime in whose middle
    tower seated
In the slight acridity you may watch
The copper thunder kept in the sulky flanks of your
    horse, a rolling field
Of necks glad to be groomed, the strong crupper, the
    edged hoof
And the long back, seductive and rebellious to saddles.
And barracks, fortresses, in need of no vest save light,
    light
That to me is breath, food and drink, I live by effects of
    light, I live
To catch it, to break it, as an orator plays off
Against each other and his theme his casual gems, and
    so with light,
Twisted in strings, plucked, crossed or knotted or
    crumbled
As it may be allowed to be by leaves,
Or clanged back by lakes and rocks or otherwise beaten,
Or else spilt and spread like a feast of honey, dripping
Through delightful voids and creeping along long
    fractures, brimming
Carved canals, bowls and lachrymatories with pearls: all
    this the work
Of now advancing, now withdrawing faces, whose use I
    know.
I know what slabs thus will be soaked to a thumb's
    depth by the sun,

And where to rob them, what colour stifles in your
    intact quarries, what
Sand silted in your river-gorges will well mix with the
    dust of flint; I know
What wood to cut by what moon in what weather
Of your sea-winds, your hill-wind: therefore tyrant, let
    me learn
Your highways, ways of sandstone, roads of the oakleaf,
    and your sea-ways.
Send me to dig dry graves, exposing what you want: I
    must
Attend your orgies and debates (let others apply for
    austerities), admit me
To your witty table, stuff me with urban levities, feed
    me, bind me
To a prudish luxury, free me thus and with a workshop
From my household consisting
Of a pregnant wife, one female and one boy child, and an
    elder bastard
With other properties; these let me regard, let me neglect,
    and let
What I begin be finished. Save me, noble sir, from the
    agony
Of starved and privy explorations such as those I stumble
From a hot bed to make, to follow lines to which the
    night-sky
Holds only faint contingencies. These flights with no end
    but failure,
And failure not to end them, these palliate or prevent.
I wish for liberty, let me then be tied: and seeing too
    much,
I aspire to be constrained by your emblems of birth and
    triumph,
And between the obligations of your future and the

checks of actual state

To flourish, adapt the stubs of an interminable descent, and place

The crested key to confident vaults; with a placid flurry of petals,

And bosom and lips, will stony functionaries support

The persuasion, so beyond proof, of your power. I will record

In peculiar scrolls your alien alliances,

Fit an apartment for your eastern hostage, extol in basalt

Your father, praise with white festoons the goddess your lady;

And for your death which will be mine prepare

An encasement as if of solid blood. And so let me

Forget, let me remember, that this is stone, stick, metal, trash

Which I will pile and hack, my hands will stain and bend

(None better knowing how to gain from the slow pains of a marble

Bruised, breathing strange climates). Being pressed as I am, being broken

By wealth and poverty, torn between strength and weakness, take me, choose

To relieve me, to receive of me, and must you not agree

As you have been to some – a great giver of banquets, of respite from swords,

Who shook out figured cloths, who rained coin;

A donor of laurel and grapes, a font of profuse intoxicants – and so,

To be so too for me? And none too soon, since the panting mind

Rather than barren will be prostitute, and once

I served a herd of merchants; but since I will be faithful

And my virtue is such, though far from home let what is

yours be mine, and this be a match
As many have been proved, enduring exiles and blazed
Not without issue in returning shows: your miserly
    freaks,
Your envies, racks and poisons not out of mind
Although not told, since often borne – indeed how
    should it be
That you employed them less than we? But now be
    flattered a little
To indulge the extravagant gist of this communication,
For my pride puts all in doubt and at present I have no
    patience,
I have simply hope, and I submit me
To your judgement which will be just.

To a Man on His Horse

Only the Arab stallion will I
Envy you. Along the water
You dance him with the morning on his flanks.
In the frosty morning that his motions flatter
He kindles, and where the winter's in the wood,
I watch you dance him out on delicate shanks.
And lashes fall on a dark eye,
He sheds a silvery mane, he shapes
His thin nostrils like a fop's.
And to do honour to his whiteness
In remembrance of his ancient blood,
I have wished to become his groom,
And so his smouldering body comb
In a simple and indecorous sweetness.

The Tears of a Muse in America

1

Call out, celebrate the beam
Imprisoning and expressing him.
Fix the mature flash for the end, but in advance
Fix in the glow of that sense what shall pass.

2

Give him a pale skin, a long hand,
A grey eye with deep eyelids, with deep lids.
Complete with a dark mouth the head
Of Veronese's equerry; though of too confident a grace
His gestures, less fine than his limbs. Allow him also to
    sleep much,
As with an effect of wantonness. Then he should swim
    and run,
Jump horses and touch music, laugh willingly and grow
Among plain manners and legalities, and yet,
Say where Monongahela and Alleghany
Have woven preparatives, glistening fall, or where
New York assembles brittle towers. And let him,
Pleased to accomplish purposes,
Alight in loose dress from a car.

3

He arrives thus with the ray of his intelligence
With what may cluster about it, dispositions
Recollections and curiosity, the state
Of reason and vision, the deceits of passion,
Play of reserves, reflections, admirations

I am luminously possessed of. And all of which am
    anxious
To acknowledge makes him another of the many-minded,
    another
Exposed and assaulted, active and passive mind,
Engaged in an adventure, and interesting and interested
In itself by so being. But here solutions bristle,
For the case seems to shine out at me from the moment
I grant him all the mind I can; when I in short
Impute to him an intemperate spirit, a proud wit
And in a springing innocence that still cannot undo itself
The pallid fire I cannot if I wish, withhold. He shall
As he does, overpraise and underprize
And outvalue and contemn all those purities and powers
Of sight and speech, the so true so rich fleece
Covertly and attentively, and often too
Fastidiously and rashly to neglect.
Here the position, action on his part, his going
In a still preserved uncertainty of light
Waits only for my touch: and there I have him
Amid the impunities of the polluted city,
I see him in the stale glare of those follies,
Illiterate illuminations run to seed,
Irreconcilables and abominables
Of all kinds swallowed, neither good nor bad
Either remembered or forgotten. In the dusk
There appears the full pallor of his looks,
Desiring and desiring to desire.
And in fine he proceeds, fanned by this dubious flush
In the way I know. It comes to me afresh,
There glimmers out of it upon me that I want
Nothing to come of it at once. It glimmers,
It glimmers from the question, of how, how shall it fall
The moment of the simple sight? and where

In what green land the simple sorrow? and
Under what boughs beneath whose hand wherever,
As in a fog upon the perfumed Cape,
A falling together of many gleams
Neither remembered nor forgotten, and neither
Undesiring nor desiring, the moment of despair?
Only say it should fall, as it will fall, as it fell
Or will have fallen, hanging back but to take place
All at once in the tacit air and on the ground
Of this period: the process
Of confrontation, reflection, resolution
That follows, it is this that will ascend
To the last point of fitted and related clarity.

4

Caught in that leisurely and transparent stream
Of the soft ostensibility of story,
His motions and his thoughts are their own net,
And while the beam folds on itself, I'll not
Deny it is indefensibly too fine.
For as in smooth seas under dawn, whatever
He does, he cannot do amiss
Being in these eyes seen aright
As he questionlessly is
In the white air under dawn
If he lives, if he dies
He but plays at all escapes
As a dolphin or salmon leaps,
And exquisite heresies
But leave the musing surface with a gleam.
So if all else be but conceivable, yet
Of a lucidity that lives, himself
Mirrored may be the same,

Antecedents and foils will palliate. For
How idly miraculous
Or of what tortuous glory,
In fact this creature was
How should my mere ingenuity relate?
In the great sweetness of which light
I ask if maybe I have made
At the last too little of it? But at least
Since I have seen him clear,
Whether he fondle a golden mare
Which he has ridden through wet woods,
Or in the sunlight by the water
Stand silent as a tree, this verse no longer weeps.

The Token

More beautiful than any gift you gave
You were, a child so beautiful as to seem
To promise ruin what no child can have,
Or woman give. And so a Roman gem
I choose to be your token: here a laurel
Springs to its young height, hangs a broken limb;
And here a group of women wanly quarrel
At a sale of Cupids. A hawk looks at them.

Soldiers Bathing

The sea at evening moves across the sand.
Under a reddening sky I watch the freedom of a band
Of soldiers who belong to me. Stripped bare
For bathing in the sea, they shout and run in the warm
    air;
Their flesh worn by the trade of war, revives
And my mind towards the meaning of it strives.

All's pathos now. The body that was gross,
Rank, ravenous, disgusting in the act or in repose,
All fever, filth and sweat, its bestial strength
And bestial decay, by pain and labour grows at length
Fragile and luminous. 'Poor bare forked animal',
Conscious of his desires and needs and flesh that rise and
    fall,
Stands in the soft air, tasting after toil
The sweetness of his nakedness: letting the sea-waves
    coil
Their frothy tongues about his feet, forgets
His hatred of the war, its terrible pressure that begets
A machinery of death and slavery,
Each being a slave and making slaves of others; finds
    that he
Remembers his old freedom in a game,
Mocking himself, and comically mimics fear and shame.

He plays with death and animality;
And reading in the shadows of his pallid flesh, I see
The idea of Michelangelo's cartoon
Of soldiers bathing, breaking off before they were half
    done
At some sortie of the enemy, an episode
Of the Pisan wars with Florence. I remember how he
    showed

Their muscular limbs that clamber from the water,
And heads that turn across the shoulder, eager for the
   slaughter,
Forgetful of their bodies that are bare,
And hot to buckle on and use the weapons lying there.
– And I think too of the theme another found
When, shadowing men's bodies on a sinister red ground,
Another Florentine, Pollaiuolo,
Painted a naked battle: warriors straddled, hacked the
   foe,
Dug their bare toes into the ground and slew
The brother-naked man who lay between their feet and
   drew
His lips back from his teeth in a grimace.

They were Italians who knew war's sorrow and disgrace
And showed the thing suspended, stripped – a theme
Born out of the experience of war's horrible extreme
Beneath a sky where even the air flows
With *lacrimae Christi*. For that rage, that bitterness, those
   blows,
That hatred of the slain, what could they be
But indirectly or directly a commentary
On the Crucifixion? And the picture burns
With indignation and pity and despair by turns,
Because it is the obverse of the scene
Where Christ hangs murdered, stripped, upon the Cross.
   I mean,
That is the explanation of its rage.

And we too have our bitterness and pity that engage
Blood, spirit in this war. But night begins,
Night of the mind: who nowadays is conscious of our
   sins?
Though every human deed concerns our blood,
And even we must know, what nobody has understood,

That some great love is over all we do,
And that is what has driven us to this fury, for so few
Can suffer all the terror of that love;
The terror of that love has set us spinning in this groove
Greased with our blood.
                                        These dry themselves and dress,
Combing their hair, forget the fear and shame of
    nakedness.
Because to love is frightening we prefer
The freedom of our crimes. Yet, as I drink the dusky
    air,
I feel a strange delight that fills me full,
Strange gratitude, as if evil itself were beautiful;
And kiss the wound in thought, while in the west
I watch a streak of red that might have issued from
    Christ's breast.

The Inn

February is the shortest month, and good
For this too, that we shall be one
With the campaigning season, and that done,
If I go where I would not by the way
I would not, on my journey I may say
That as it was, it will be; and I should
Come back the way I would to where I would.

Royal marriages were celebrated so,
Before the year's intrigues began.
A royal woman and a man
Were joined like puppets to beget a love
Imputed by the plot, and set to move
Apart, together; as you come, I go
To the unknown the way I do not know:

That's in your arms, where now you know, and why
The war will happen for this year,
And we between us get and bear
Whatever is to be when we have been;
So you may not be but the winter-queen
Of schism in Bohemia, nor I
Elector of an exile where I'll die.

With politics like these the war uncharms
Our new-born marriage, that must learn
Such days as these that now return,
Are torn, and are to tear us. O but first,
We will lodge here: the weather may be curst,
But here's the inn; no manger but my arms,
Where none but you or I can do us harms.

The Question

And so we too came where the rest have come,
To where each dreamed, each drew, the other home
From all distractions to the other's breast;
Where each had found, each was, the wild bird's nest.
For that we came, and knew that we must know
The thing we knew of but we did not know.

We said then, What if this were now no more
Than a faint shade of what we thought before?
If love should here find little joy, or none,
And done, it were as if it were not done;
Would we not love still? What if none can know
The thing we know of but we do not know?

For we know nothing but that, long ago
We learnt to love God whom we cannot know.
I touch your eyelids that one day must close,
Your lips as perishable as a rose;
And say that all must fade before we know
The thing we know of but we do not know.

The Old Age of Michelangelo

Sometimes the light falls here too as at Florence
Circled by low hard hills, or in the quarry
Under its half-hewn cliffs, where that collection
Of pale rough blocks, still lying at all angles on the
    dust-white floor
Waits, like a town of tombs.
                        I finish nothing I begin.
And the dream sleeps in the stone, to be unveiled
Or half-unveiled, the lurking nakedness;
Luminous as a grapeskin, the cold marble mass
Of melted skeins, chains, veils and veins,
Bosses and hollows, muscular convexities,
Supple heroic surfaces, tense drums
And living knots and cords of love:
 – Sleeps in the stone, and is unveiled
Or half-unveiled, the body's self a veil,
By the adze and the chisel, and the mind
Impelled by torment.
                  In the empty quarry
The light waits, and the tombs wait,
For the coming of a dream.

*

The power with which I imagine makes these things,
This prison.
And while the dream stirs in the stone, wakes in its
    chains,
Sometimes I think that I have spent my whole life
    making tombs,
And even those are unfinished. And yet, chafing,
Sadly closed there, in a rich bare case

Of bodily loveliness like solid sleep,
One sees the soul that turns
Waking, stretched on her side as if in pain, and how she
    sees
Browed like the dawn, the dark world
 – Like a sulky pale cold louring dawn –
Loathing her hope of fruit, the pure bare flank:
Or else one sees her sunk in rest,
Letting her worn head droop over her empty body
And the much-pulled breasts hang dry,
Fallen, with long flat nipples.

And there is always
Some victor and some vanquished, always the fierce
    substance
And the divine idea, a drunkenness
Of high desire and thought, or a stern sadness:
And while it rests or broods or droops,
There will be always some great arm or shoulder
To incur or to impose some heavy torment,
There will be always the great self on guard, the giant
Reclined and ominous,
With back half-turned, hunched shoulder
And the enormous thigh
Drawn up as if disdainful,
Almost the bare buttock offered:
There will be always
A tall Victory with beaten Age
Doubled beneath its bent knee, but ignoring
(The naked proud youth bending aside
His vacuous burning brow and wide
Beautiful eyes and blank lips) but ignoring
The sad sordid slave, the old man.

*

And now I have grown old,
It is my own life, my long life I see
As a combat against nature, nature that is our enemy
Holding the soul a prisoner by the heel;
And my whole anxious life I see
As a combat with myself, that I do violence to myself,
To bruise and beat and batter
And bring under
My own being,
Which is an infinite savage sea of love.

*

For you must know I am of all men ever born
Most inclined to love persons, and whenever I see
    someone
Who has gifts of mind and body, and can say or show
    me something
Better than the rest,
Straightway I am compelled
To fall in love with him, and then I give myself
Up to him so completely, I belong no longer to myself,
He wresting from me
So great part of my being, I am utterly
Bewildered and distraught, and for many days know
    nothing
Of what I am doing or where I am.

– Young green wood spits in burning,
Dry wood catches the flame; and I become now
An old man with a face like wrinkled leather, living
    alone,
And with no friends but servants,

Parasites, bad disciples puffed up by my favours, or else
  Popes,
Kings, cardinals or other patrons, being as for myself
  alone
Either a lord or subject, either with my gossips and
  buffoons
And clumsy fawning relatives; or towards you and such
  as you,
Whom I adore, an abject:
                    Messer THOMAS
CAVALIERE
I am naked in that sea of love
Which is an infinite savage glowing sea,
Where I must sink or swim. Cold, burning with sorrow,
I am naked in that sea and know
The sad foam of the restless flood
Which floats the soul or kills, and I have swum there
These fifty years and more,
And never have I burned and frozen
More than I have for you,
Messer Tommaso.

                    *

Moon-cold or sun-hot, through what alternations
Of energy, long languor,
Periods of mad defiance, periods of fear, flight, misery
Cowering darkly,
Moon-cold or sun-hot, love that grips
Sun, moon, eternal hatred
Eternal hope and pain, packed close in one man's body,
And drawn, leaning to others.
                    And one other:
Grey eyes float in the dry light
That might draw Venus' car, moving at morning

Grey eyes through dry dark shadows, floating
Over the blocked ways, the despair,
And opening wide lids, irises
More starlike than the stars, purer than they, alive in the
    pale air,
Fire, life in thin dry air
Drawing the soul out at the mouth
Beauty in triumph,
My defeat.

*

– I am always alone, I speak to no one
But that shabby Bernardo, nor do I wish to:
Trudging up and down Italy, wearing out my shoes and
    life,
Toiling still to grow poorer, ugly, sad,
Proud, narrow, full of unfulfilled desires!

Yet I have come to Rome, rich in its ruins, and for the
    last time,
As if I made to cross a little stream dry-foot
That had divided us, and yet again, for the last time
My dream grows drunk within me,
And opens its great wings and like an eagle
Wild naked perfect pure, soars from its nest.
Almost I am persuaded, almost, that it is possible,
My love, like anybody's love, is possible.
My eye stares on your face, and my old mind
Soars naked from its cliff, and thinks to find
– Drunk with illumination as the sky itself is drunken
Or a dry river-bed with light –
The wild path to its thought, for all is passion
Here, even cogitation, and it climbs and clambers,
    floats and flings

And hovers, it is thrust up, it is hurled
Throbbing into the stillness,
Rapt, carried by the blissful air
Borne up, rebuffs and buffets
 – Having hurled
The dead world far below it –
Stretches out long rapturous claws and wings,
Stiff as with agony, shakes as with tenderness
And dives and hovers at you, swoops and aches
To stun, caress
And beat you to your knees,
Clutches and clings,

 – As if it would grow one with you and carry
Up the solitary sky
That strange new beautiful identity,
Where it might never fade or melt or die!
And many things
Are put about and taken up and spread abroad
About Michelangelo, poor old man, but when I
Come to you, I care nothing
For honour or the world, I only care
To look long on your face, and let
The dream soar from its nest. For do I know
Myself, what I should mean? I only know
That if I had those wings, not in a dream,
And I could open, beat those wings;
If I could clutch you in the claws of dream,
And take you up with me in loneliness
To the roof-tree, angle of heaven, vault
Of exquisite pale buffeted glare:
I should gain or regain
The heaven of that high passion, pallor, innocence

– I should gain or regain
The sole pure love, and fence it with my wings.

*

But my two eyes
Are empty, having wept, and my skin stretched
Like an old hide over dry bones, and my face
Grown flat and timorous, broken,
Loving or having loved this dream.
And the light fades from the sky, the dream dies in the
    stone
Slowly, I finish nothing I begin, and in my evening
Last torments and last light, torn hesitations
Between desire and fear, between desire and my disdain
– Emerging into dusky rooms, high halls, rich
    architecture
And the tawny roofs of Rome. For this love discovers
    only
The world's desert and death, the dusty prison
Where we have shut ourselves, or the sky shuts us.

Fades the light, and below there
I lie, an old man like a fallen god propped up:
My eyes close, and my head hangs,
Heavy as if with love-drink or with dreams,
And from my old thick swagging side
Pours forth a marble river. Overhead floats
A face, two brilliant eyes
That make the whole world pale,
Floating, and that great nobleness,
That great despising, of the mind
To which the beautiful is as the felt heat
Of the fire of the eternal.

Do not forget the poor old man.

Watching Song

1

Watch, I warn you,
By night and starlight,
You who are chosen to
Stand on the brick-built
Walls of Modena:
Wait for the dawn-hour.

2

Standing at arms and
Peering in darkness
Over the flatlands;
Pacing slowly
On open stretches
Of mortared levels or
Close in catwalks;
Pause and listen,
With lowered eyelid and
Heart under breastplate:
Question the silence.

3

– Nothing but frogs
That chatter in ditches,
And crying of nightbirds.
Yet we watch to
Outwit the sorrowful,
Shag-haired rabble of
Heathen raiders.

4

And so in our sentries
Bound and helmeted,
Over the city
We sing our watches,
Call on the Name and
Summon our safety –
Singing in antiphon,
Answer in unison,
'Lord God omnipotent,
Shield and companion:

5

'Saviour and King,
And crown of mankind;
You who were born for
Our peace, to stand over us,
Keep your hand over us.'

6

Then, as the song goes,
Hear it echoing
Round by the walls
Of the guarded city,
Floating by tenements,
Roofs and courtyards,
Domes of churches and
Empty markets –
Stirring and comforting
Drowsy families,
Strangers at inns and
Close-laid lovers:
The patient candle

Of cellared workmen
Yawning at benches:
Shuttered taverns,
And prayers in silence,
And lamps by altars
That live in darkness.

7

Then watch together, singing together
And stand as faithful,
Hearing it echo
Round by the walls we
Keep in safety,
Until the first breath
Sent from the dawn-hour
Touches the night's face,
And the dawn brightens.

Les Congés du Lépreux

Plague and sores beyond relief
Have pierced me, skin and bone.
I must set up house with grief,
And travel hence alone.
Death has forced me to content
And with a darkness buys me day;
Poverty has paid my rent,
And counts tomorrow for today.
Pity, with those two red eyes,
And sorrow, looking back on me,
Do these errands I devise
To friends whom I shall never see.

One who taught me how to write,
Gerard of Pontlouvain,
Pity, waft what I indite,
And weep, if it be plain.
What he taught me, now I find
Serviceable to my pain,
So beyond my scabby rind
I touch his friendship yet again.
Now there's nothing sweet or sound
Left about me, but my heart,
Sorrow, as you go your round,
Give him that, and so depart.

Those who catered to my woes
When I was going rotten,
Sorrow, thank, but also those
By whom they were forgotten.
They relieved my body once,
And gave it pleasure in their hour,

And the body I renounce;
But I would not be rude or sour.
Go and tell old Simon Hall,
Now that I peel from head to feet,
With his good men by the wall
I can no longer sit at meat.

Pity, you may say goodbye
To two more I shall miss,
Hugo and Bertyl, and thereby
Look pale, and tell them this:
They may sail for Palestine,
As I had done, and made up three;
With their cross they can carry mine;
The pagans have a truce, for me.
God has quit me of my vow,
I owe no ransom for release.
Say that I go with them now,
Although I die at home in peace.

Mortimer

March has flooded meadows,
Spring comes in a gale.
Ploughlands and bare hedges
Are bullied, and the pale
Gold willow-wands
Toss by the beaten ponds.

And now I am tormented
By such gap of loss
As this love can bring;
And the wind drops, and across
The russet lands,
Sad spring a moment stands.

Budding sweetness yet
Haunts that lack of breath:
The osiers and hazels
And alders, flush in death,
And a bird cries
To open the dull skies.

from *Strambotti*

i

I wish there were a passage underground
That led by magic to your house and bed,
So I could be beside you at a bound,
When I had made the journey in my head.
Then I should disappear and not be found,
And neighbours be persuaded I were dead;
But I should be with you in Paradise,
Where I could laugh, and kiss your face and eyes.

ii

If I could conjure shapes for you and me,
I'd choose two living things that swim or fly,
Two fishes tumbling in a glassy sea,
Two eagles turning in a golden sky;
And in those shapes we should continue free,
And still in love, until the sea ran dry,
The air failed, and the earth dropped in the sun,
And time was ended, and we two were one.

iii

Wanting more courage than a wandering knight
Led by adventures on from place to place,
Like him, if I should waver I do right
To gaze in silence on my lover's face:
For that pale oval shadow can make light
In my account, of danger and disgrace;
And if they were to come I would not yield,
If I could have it painted on my shield.

iv

Counting the heavy days and heavy hours,
I measure out the prison of this town,
And wear out stones with that desire of
    ours,
But not desire, by walking up and down.
And you are like a city full of towers,
Set by a plain or river like a crown;
And you are like a sunset and a star;
But I am here alone, not where you are.

v

Love and good luck breathed on the builder's
    hand
When he took thought and set the window so,
And set it facing where the bed may stand,
And every day the sun will rise and show:
For when the sun is rising as he planned,
With it a gentle wind begins to blow,
And darkness and the stars fade out above;
But your two open eyes are stars of love.

vi

And we are two, but neither tall nor short,
And equally in love in heart and mind;
And we are like two pillars of one fort,
Of equal faith, and equally combined.
And we are two, but one in every sort,
If ever there were such among mankind;
And others who have wished, alive or
    dead,
To lie together in one grave, or bed.

vii

LETTER

Coming to write my letter, overcast
By all the days of absence that have gone,
I think of others passing as they passed –
So many days of sun that never shone,
Letters and days! And this is not the last,
And I must doubt, to see them stretching on;
And I must wonder if it would be strange,
Sooner or later, for our love to change.

And yet I know our luck has won the toss
So many times! and most of all that day
When your first letter came and chanced to cross
One I had ventured – half-afraid to say
What I felt suddenly, in dread of loss;
And then your letter came, and in a way
Said less, but it could only be a sign! ...
– And so it all comes back, to breathe and shine,

And so I run it through, how love began:
The slight encounter, while we hardly thought,
And pleasant company without a plan;
But then the wild desire, and we were caught!
How then we were afraid, and blight and ban
Had clawed at us like devils – but we fought,
And in the end won sweetness from it all;
And how that would be sweeter to recall.

And surely we will call it up again
One day, and laugh to see it shine and sing –
Know it is not a dream, but true and plain,
And we shall never find a better thing!

Then we shall bless what we have bought with pain,
And close it like the two halves of a ring.
– But now I only tell my letter, go;
And say I wish that I could travel so.

Autumn Journey

I saw from the gliding train
A yellow birch in the woods below,
And the dark pines close in again,
And thought of dry leaves falling slow
Under the cold cloud-shadows,
Horses of shadow, loosed in dreams;
And of the Snow Queen, pale and fair,
And Gerda looking for her Kay,
Poor Gerda, when she met the crow
Who led her in by the back way:
So, as they climbed the castle stair
To reach the bedroom where he lay,
Dark horses plunged like shadows,
Long-legged on the wall, in dreams;
And Gerda, while her heart beat fast,
Came where he slept, half turned away,
And called him, and the dreams rushed past,
And he awoke, and was not Kay.

Sea View

Sunlight catches a wall,
It glows, and I recall,
Ten years ago, our walk,
And how we sat to stare,
Quite happy not to talk,
Blown by the mild sea air:
The bench in wind and sun
Above the pearl-grey sea,
Perched on the broken cliff,
The joy, the strange fragility –
Precarious, conscious, pleased –
The youth in everything,
Sweet, and yet not appeased
By all our love could bring.

And then the sunny quay,
The ferry churning clear,
Gulls idling on the sea,
And there, along the pier
The little trundling train!
No doubt it trundles on,
As I do, but again
Grown sad that you are gone.

from *Memoirs in Oxford*

i

The sun shines on the gliding river,
　The river shines and presses through
Damp meadows and just yellowing trees;
The tall trees left without a breeze
　Stand up against the blue!

And on one side a space for cows is
　Fenced off, with willow-stumps and wires;
While there the place of learning drowses –
Churches and colleges and houses
　Lifting their domes and towers and spires.

I can remember coming here
　For the first time, and in the sun
Of such an autumn, gold and clear;
I walked alone – it was the year
　Of 'crisis', nineteen thirty-one.

Frenchmen were wearing in lapels
　Ne me parlez pas de la crise!
Nobody could foresee what hells
Were waiting – some were forming cells,
　Others could be at ease;

But one could feel the chill on stricken
　England like an eclipse at noon –
A ghostly twilight come to sicken
The old bewildered realm, and thicken
　To darkness and disaster soon.

Yet here am I, and forced to try
  Thirty years later as it is,
To find some way of telling all –
So, pacing by a mossy wall
  Think of the opportunities

I missed! And can I now forgive
  Myself for having missed so much?
I was afraid to take or give –
Disabled or unfit, to live
  And love – reach out and touch.

*

It hangs in sunlight now past change
  And what is worse, beyond disguise.
That past I meet is looking strange;
But I must welcome it, arrange
  The meeting – and allow no lies.

Old faded photographs can so
  Look new to us; and I have one
Here of my mother, I can show –
I took it all those years ago
  Nearby in the December sun.

Dressed warmly, with her touch and sense
  Of rightness, by the elm-tree bole
She stands: too calm to be called 'tense',
Yet some defiance or defence
  Looks out of her from top to sole.

It must have been my second year.
  One sees the pang that all along

She had suppressed – and more was here,
More on the way; she looks quite clear
  On that; and she would not be wrong.

Not that I grant her prophecy
  Of even how the world would go!
And some black cards for her and me
The pack held, that she could not see –
  Some she would never know.

But she might ask what had translated
  A nature ardent and direct
In childhood – leaving it self-hated,
Involved, remote; and what awaited
  The boy she could not now protect?

I could not tell but had to live
  The change, and suffer: cold, confined,
Withholding what I longed to give –
The love I craved – a sensitive
  Of the most complicated kind.

ii

My father from the time I claim
  Remembrance, on his mantelshelf
Had standing always in the same
Silver and dark-blue velvet frame
  A small old photograph of himself:

At twenty, at his most beautiful –
  Long-jacketed, pale-faced, dark-eyed!
Like a young moon that nears the full
And gazes on a twilight pool,
  His head was tilted to one side.

I had left home before he died,
   Young as the picture showed him then.
Afterwards – sore, unsatisfied –
I begged it, and was not denied;
   But it had gone, no one knew when

Or where! And I recall the room,
   The silence; no one spoke because
Everyone saw the question loom:
'He had given it, but – to whom?'
   We held our breath and left the pause.

*

My mother blamed his education
   For faults and lessons never learned:
His puns and self-depreciation;
Wrong choice of friends, and speculation –
   Gambling with money so well-earned!

Thinking himself a common man
   He gave himself with too much trust;
Stubborn in weakness, dumb in pride –
His deepest hopes unsatisfied
   Were apt to end in self-disgust.

I had adored, then hatefully
   Rejected him – in an immense
Hard rage and boyish misery;
Yet now in all he was I see
   A strange and saving innocence.

I grieve that we were never friends –
   It hurts; but neither would know how.
What that I say can make amends?

I leave it, knowing how it ends,
   And love him as I see him now.

For now he is beyond our reach
   I share and understand too well –
And let his love of music teach
Me, like a touch not needing speech –
   Things he could never tell.

*

But I must thank my mother's mind,
   Her fiery rational sense of right
And love of all things well-designed,
Books, furniture and people – signed
   With logic, courage, wit and light.

She gave us pictures and adventures,
   Ballads and stories by the fire,
Echoes of Ruskin and Carlyle,
The notion that there could be 'style';
   But most, herself and her desire.

She *was* Jane Eyre and Maggie Tulliver,
   Those ardent women! only free,
After such hardships – childhood scrapes,
Young visions, efforts and escapes –
   As in the mind's eye we could see:

And we were Oliver and Jim
   Hawkins and David Copperfield;
And Absalom with gold hair in
The Bible, and young Benjamin,
   And Jairus' daughter that was healed.

So old, so battered and forlorn
    I might have seemed at twenty-one!
A breathing body yet unborn,
Or blown, and withering on the thorn –
    Ten poor enigmas tied in one.

*

If in another time and place
    With other accidents I can
Conceive myself – but can one know it? –
Not mad enough to be a poet
    But a successful active man –

Engineer, architect or lawyer:
    – How can one think the self away
Or feel identity could change?
Yet occupations to estrange
    Me less, might well have come my way.

But above others hard to seek
    Instead, of all most difficult
The kingdom that I chose was weak,
Neglected, poor – the way oblique
    And quite uncertain of result.

– It was no choice, I could not choose!
    Much rather had it caught me, pinned
Or pinioned by a leash, a bond
Of cobweb, to a thought beyond
    This earth and sea, and sun and wind –

Dying and burning in faint fire,
    As if spring feared to come and trod

Half-cowering, shivering in desire
And naked in that thin attire
   Of bud and twig and dusty clod ...

For so I figure it, as weak –
   Uncertain – but a thing 'of might',
A thread that leads to the abyss
Of love and death. And it was this
   That held me, drew to harder sight:

Held me half-blinded by my need,
   Or by slow torment drew me on –
Forced me to know myself and heed
My own necessities indeed;
   Yet when I summoned it – was gone.

iv

Plato says that in Heaven there is
   Laid up the pattern of a city
Which the man who desires it sees;
And he can follow its decrees
   And live in justice, truth and pity.

Whether it does or ever will
   Exist, that city, is another
Matter: the man who sees it still
Can live according to its will,
   And be subject to no other.

Nothing could on the face of it
   Be less like my experience
Than Plato's claim – that I admit;
And yet it can be made to fit
   I think, the glimpse I had, the sense

Of that 'poor kingdom'. There it stood
　　Waiting, if one but stopped and groped –
Waiting; for one who never came,
Or passed – the empty path – a name . . .
　　And some were dead who loved and hoped:

– Or as a lamp shines on a ceiling,
　　The curtains wide; through foggy night
One sees it from the country lane,
Feels quiet warm life behind the pane –
　　There if one could decide aright,

There if one *would*! . . . It was the hope
　　Within my hope, that gave it wings:
However it may sound obscure
The thing itself is clear and sure –
　　Not the exigencies it brings.

*

– Or so I think this afternoon,
　　And passing through a Roman arch
Of yellow stone vermiculated,
Sit down and ponder in belated
　　Sunshine, by a tuft of larch.

The gardens are for birds in bushes
　　And one slow fountain; walled in stone,
And set on low ground by the river,
They shelter – though the tree-tops quiver
　　Continually, lightly blown.

So light a stir will not deter
　　The bees which are intent on going

Through that wisteria on the wall;
The sprays of blossom break and fall
   And dangle – honey-scented, glowing.

And yet their delicate mauve clusters
   Even in this good year are muffled
By that peculiar silky pale
Brown foliage; they had been too frail
   To come without it, chilled and ruffled.

You must have seen a plant like this,
   In some strange climate but assuming
The task of being what it is –
Spreading and budding, not to miss
   The happiness of blooming.

Finally it is rich and sweet –
   Spills, offers up the incense hoarded
Through penury – the robe it spun
Floats and is starry in the sun;
   All that was drab or sad and sordid

Melts into light! And looked at so,
   Of course the plant has come together
With life, thought, impulse – all one sees
As lasting through our century's
   Long tale of broken weather.

*

For so we live it out displaced,
   And caught by every wind that blows –
Revolt, mere flatulence or waste;
Terror – confusion – loveless haste
   And malice reaping as it sows:

And all these things can blast the spirit
   And leave it old, and ill, and mad!
But I survived and persevered,
Even had luck, as it appeared;
   So I was given – what I had.

And that was – well, what any man
   At times, and even the dead world knows,
And every line should have conveyed:
If not, it is too late – they fade,
   The wind drops and the sunlight goes,

And I can only moralize
   What Plato said. There was a vision –
Verse, music – but the centre lies
Beyond; and my wisteria tries,
   Lives and will die – the soul in prison –

To give itself in love and light!
   Which if we do, the rest is 'sent' –
Nothing that comes can come amiss,
No evil, loss or pain. And this
   May be what Plato meant.

STEPHEN SPENDER

'Not to you I sighed.
No, not a word . . .'

Not to you I sighed. No, not a word.
We climbed together. Any feeling was
Formed with the hills. It was like trees' unheard
And monumental sign of country peace.

But next day, stumbling, panting up dark stairs,
Rushing in room and door flung wide, I knew.
Oh empty walls, book-carcases, blank chairs
All splintered in my head and cried for you.

'*Acts passed beyond the boundary of mere wishing . . .*'

Acts passed beyond the boundary of mere wishing
Not privy looks, hedged words, at times you saw.
These, blundering, heart-surrendered troopers were
Small presents made, and waiting for the tram.
Then once you said: 'Waiting was very kind',
And looked surprised. Surprising for me, too,
Whose every movement had been missionary,
A pleading tongue unheard. I had not thought
That you, who nothing else saw, would see this.

So 'very kind' was merest overflow
Something I had not reckoned in myself,
A chance deserter from my force. When we touched
    hands,
I felt the whole rebel, feared mutiny
And turned away,
Thinking, if these were tricklings through a dam,
I must have love enough to run a factory on,
Or give a city power, or drive a train.

'*An 'I' can never*
be great man . . .'

An 'I' can never be great man.
This known great one has weakness
To friends is most remarkable for weakness:
His ill-temper at meals, dislike of being contradicted,
His only real pleasure fishing in ponds,
His only real wish – forgetting.

To advance from friends to the composite self,
Central 'I' is surrounded by 'I eating',
'I loving', 'I angry', 'I excreting',
And the great 'I' planted in him
Has nothing to do with all these,

Can never claim its true place
Resting in the forehead, and calm in his gaze.
The great 'I' is an unfortunate intruder
Quarrelling with 'I tiring' and 'I sleeping'
And all those other 'I's who long for 'We dying'.

'My parents kept me from
children who were rough . . .'

My parents kept me from children who were rough
Who threw words like stones and who wore torn clothes.
Their thighs showed through rags. They ran in the street
And climbed cliffs and stripped by the country streams.

I feared more than tigers their muscles like iron
Their jerking hands and their knees tight on my arms.
I feared the salt coarse pointing of those boys
Who copied my lisp behind me on the road.

They were lithe, they sprang out behind hedges
Like dogs to bark at my world. They threw mud
While I looked the other way, pretending to smile.
I longed to forgive them, but they never smiled.

'What I expected, was . . .'

What I expected, was
Thunder, fighting,
Long struggles with men
And climbing.
After continual straining
I should grow strong;
Then the rocks would shake,
And I rest long.

What I had not foreseen
Was the gradual day
Weakening the will
Leaking the brightness away,
The lack of good to touch,
The fading of body and soul
– Smoke before wind,
Corrupt, unsubstantial.

The wearing of Time,
And the watching of cripples pass
With limbs shaped like questions
In their odd twist,
The pulverous grief
Melting the bones with pity,
The sick falling from earth –
These, I could not foresee.

Expecting always
Some brightness to hold in trust,
Some final innocence
Except from dust,
That, hanging solid,

Would dangle through all,
Like the created poem,
Or faceted crystal.

'Who live under the shadow
of a war...'

Who live under the shadow of a war,
What can I do that matters?
My pen stops, and my laughter, dancing, stop,
Or ride to a gap.

How often, on the powerful crest of pride,
I am shot with thought
That halts the untamed horses of the blood,
The grip on good;

That moving, whimpering, and mating, bear
Tunes to deaf ears:
Stuffed with the realer passions of the earth
Beneath this hearth.

'Without that once clear aim,
the path of flight ...'

Without that once clear aim, the path of flight
To follow for a lifetime through white air,
This century chokes me under roots of night.
I suffer like history in Dark Ages, where
Truth lies in dungeons, too deep for whisper.
We hear of towers long broken off from sight
And tortures and wars, smoky and dark with rumour,
But on the buried Mind there falls no light.
Watch me who walk through coiling streets where rain
And fog choke every sigh; round corners of day,
Road-drills explore new areas of pain,
Nor trees reach leaf-lit branches down to play.
The city climbs in horror to my brain,
The writings are my only wings away.

'I think continually of those
who were truly great . . .'

I think continually of those who were truly great.
Who, from the womb, remembered the soul's history
Through corridors of light where the hours are suns,
Endless and singing. Whose lovely ambition
Was that their lips, still touched with fire,
Should tell of the Spirit, clothed from head to foot in
  song.
And who hoarded from the Spring branches
The desires falling across their bodies like blossoms.

What is precious, is never to forget
The essential delight of the blood drawn from ageless
  springs
Breaking through rocks in worlds before our earth.
Never to deny its pleasure in the morning simple light
Nor its grave evening demand for love.
Never to allow gradually the traffic to smother
With noise and fog, the flowering of the Spirit.

Near the snow, near the sun, in the highest fields,
See how these names are fêted by the waving grass
And by the streamers of white cloud
And whispers of wind in the listening sky.
The names of those who in their lives fought for life,
Who wore at their hearts the fire's centre.
Born of the sun, they travelled a short while toward the
  sun
And left the vivid air signed with their honour.

The Express

After the first powerful, plain manifesto
The black statement of pistons, without more fuss
But gliding like a queen, she leaves the station.
Without bowing and with restrained unconcern
She passes the houses which humbly crowd outside,
The gasworks, and at last the heavy page
Of death, printed by gravestones in the cemetery.
Beyond the town, there lies the open country
Where, gathering speed, she acquires mystery,
The luminous self-possession of ships on ocean.
It is now she begins to sing – at first quite low
Then loud, and at last with a jazzy madness –
The song of her whistle screaming at curves,
Of deafening tunnels, brakes, innumerable bolts.
And always light, aerial, underneath,
Retreats the elate metre of her wheels.
Steaming through metal landscape on her lines,
She plunges new eras of white happiness,
Where speed throws up strange shapes, broad curves
And parallels clean like trajectories from guns.
At last, further than Edinburgh or Rome,
Beyond the crest of the world, she reaches night
Where only a low stream-line brightness
Of phosphorus on the tossing hills is light.
Ah, like a comet through flame, she moves entranced,
Wrapt in her music no bird song, no, nor bough
Breaking with honey buds, shall ever equal.

The Pylons

The secret of these hills was stone, and cottages
Of that stone made,
And crumbling roads
That turned on sudden hidden villages.

Now over these small hills, they have built the concrete
That trails black wire;
Pylons, those pillars
Bare like nude giant girls that have no secret.

The valley with its gilt and evening look
And the green chestnut
Of customary root,
Are mocked dry like the parched bed of a brook.

But far above and far as sight endures
Like whips of anger
With lightning's danger
There runs the quick perspective of the future.

This dwarfs our emerald country by its trek
So tall with prophecy:
Dreaming of cities
Where often clouds shall lean their swan-white neck.

An Elementary School Classroom
in a Slum

Far far from gusty waves these children's faces.
Like rootless weeds, the hair torn round their pallor.
The tall girl with her weighed-down head. The paper-
seeming boy, with rat's eyes. The stunted, unlucky heir
Of twisted bones, reciting a father's gnarled disease,
His lesson from his desk. At back of the dim class
One unnoted, sweet and young. His eyes live in a dream
Of squirrel's game, in tree room, other than this.

On sour cream walls, donations. Shakespeare's head,
Cloudless at dawn, civilized dome riding all cities.
Belled, flowery, Tyrolese valley. Open-handed map
Awarding the world its world. And yet, for these
Children, these windows, not this world, are world,
Where all their future's painted with a fog,
A narrow street sealed in with a lead sky,
Far far from rivers, capes and stars of words.

Surely, Shakespeare is wicked, the map a bad example
With ships and sun and love tempting them to steal –
For lives that slyly turn in their cramped holes
From fog to endless night? On their slag heap, these
   children
Wear skins peeped through by bones and spectacles of
   steel
With mended glass, like bottle bits on stones.
All of their time and space are foggy slum.
So blot their maps with slums as big as doom.

Unless, governor, teacher, inspector, visitor,
This map becomes their window and these windows

That shut upon their lives like catacombs,
Break O break open till they break the town
And show the children to green fields, and make their
　　world
Run azure on gold sands, and let their tongues
Run naked into books, the white and green leaves open
History theirs whose language is the sun.

A Footnote

(From Marx's Chapter, *The Working Day*)

'Heard say that four times four is eight,'
'And the King is the Man what has all the Gold.'
'Our King is a Queen and her son's a Princess
'And they live in a Palace called London, I'm told.'

'Heard say that a man called God who's a Dog
'Made the World, with us in it.' 'And then I've heard
'There came a great Flood and the World was all
    drowned
'Except for one Man, and he was a Bird.'

'So perhaps all the People are dead, and we're Birds
'Shut in steel cages by the Devil, who's good,
'Like the Miners in their pit cages
'And us in our Chimneys to climb, as we should.'

– Ah, twittering voices
Of children crawling on their knees
Through notes of Blue Books, History Books,
At foot of the most crowded pages,
You are the birds of a songless age
Young like the youngest gods, awarded
Mythical childhood always.
Stunted spirits in a fog
Weaving the land
Into tapestries of smoke,
You whisper among wheels
Calling to your stripped and sacred mothers
With straps tied round their waists
For dragging trucks along a line.

In the sunset above London
Often I watch you lean upon the clouds
Drawn back like a curtain –
O cupids and cherubim
Fixed in the insensate eye
Of a tragic, ignorant age.

Two Armies

Deep in the winter plain, two armies
Dig their machinery, to destroy each other.
Men freeze and hunger. No one is given leave
On either side, except the dead, and wounded.
These have their leave; while new battalions wait
On time at last to bring them violent peace.

All have become so nervous and so cold
That each man hates the cause and distant words
That brought him here, more terribly than bullets.
Once a boy hummed a popular marching song,
Once a novice hand flapped their salute;
The voice was choked, the lifted hand fell,
Shot through the wrist by those of his own side.

From their numb harvest, all would flee, except
For discipline drilled once in an iron school
Which holds them at the point of the revolver.
Yet when they sleep, the images of home
Ride wishing horses of escape
Which herd the plain in a mass unspoken poem.

Finally, they cease to hate: for although hate
Bursts from the air and whips the earth with hail
Or shoots it up in fountains to marvel at,
And although hundreds fall, who can connect
The inexhaustible anger of the guns
With the dumb patience of those tormented animals?

Clean silence drops at night, when a little walk
Divides the sleeping armies, each
Huddled in linen woven by remote hands.

When the machines are stilled, a common suffering
Whitens the air with breath and makes both one
As though these enemies slept in each other's arms.

Only the lucid friend to aerial raiders
The brilliant pilot moon, stares down
Upon this plain she makes a shining bone
Cut by the shadows of many thousand bones.
Where amber clouds scatter on No-Man's-Land
She regards death and time throw up
The furious words and minerals which destroy.

Ultima Ratio Regum

The guns spell money's ultimate reason
In letters of lead on the Spring hillside.
But the boy lying dead under the olive trees
Was too young and too silly
To have been notable to their important eye.
He was a better target for a kiss.

When he lived, tall factory hooters never summoned him
Nor did restaurant plate-glass doors revolve to wave him
    in
His name never appeared in the papers.
The world maintained its traditional wall
Round the dead with their gold sunk deep as a well,
Whilst his life, intangible as a Stock Exchange rumour,
    drifted outside.

O too lightly he threw down his cap
One day when the breeze threw petals from the trees.
The unflowering wall sprouted with guns,
Machine-gun anger quickly scythed the grasses;
Flags and leaves fell from hands and branches;
The tweed cap rotted in the nettles.

Consider his life which was valueless
In terms of employment, hotel ledgers, news files.
Consider. One bullet in ten thousand kills a man.
Ask. Was so much expenditure justified
On the death of one so young, and so silly
Lying under the olive trees, O world, O death?

Port Bou

As a child holds a pet
Arms clutching but with hands that do not join
And the coiled animal looks through the gap
To outer freedom animal air,
So the earth-and-rock arms of this small harbour
Embrace but do not encircle the sea
Which, through a gap, vibrates into the ocean,
Where dolphins swim and liners throb.
In the bright winter sunlight I sit on the parapet
Of a bridge; my circling arms rest on a newspaper
And my mind is empty as the glittering stone
While I search for an image
(The one written above) and the words (written above)
To set down the childish headlands of Port Bou.
A lorry halts beside me with creaking brakes
And I look up at warm downwards-looking faces
Of militia men staring at my (French) newspaper.
'How do they write of our struggle over the frontier?'
I hold out the paper, but they cannot read it,
They want speech and to offer cigarettes.
In their waving flag-like faces the war finds peace. The
famished mouths
Of rusted carbines lean against their knees.
Wrapped in cloth – old granny in a shawl –
The stuttering machine-gun rests.
They shout – salute back as the truck jerks forward
Over the vigorous hill, beyond the headland.
An old man passes, his mouth dribbling,
From three rusted teeth, he shoots out: 'pom-pom-pom'.
The children run after; and, more slowly, the women;
Clutching their skirts, trail over the horizon.
Now Port Bou is empty, for the firing practice.

I am left alone on the parapet at the exact centre
Above the river trickling through the gully, like that
    old man's saliva.
The exact centre, solitary as the bull's eye in a target.
Nothing moves against the background of stage-scenery
    houses
Save the skirring mongrels. The firing now begins
Across the harbour mouth, from headland to headland,
White flecks of foam whipped by lead from the sea.
An echo spreads its cat-o'-nine tails
Thrashing the flanks of neighbour hills.
My circling arms rest on the newspaper,
My mind is paper on which dust and words sift,
I assure myself the shooting is only for practice
But I am the coward of cowards. The machine-gun
    stitches
My intestines with a needle, back and forth;
The solitary, spasmodic, white puffs from the carbines
Draw fear in white threads back and forth through my
    body.

The Double Shame

You must live through the time when everything hurts
When the space of the ripe, loaded afternoon
Expands to a landscape of white heat frozen
And trees are weighed down with hearts of stone
And green stares back where you stare alone,
And the walking eyes throw flinty comments,
And the words which carry most knives are the blind
Phrases searching to be kind.

Solid and usual objects are ghosts
The furniture carries cargoes of memory,
The staircase has corners which remember
As fire blows reddest in gusty embers,
And each empty dress cuts out an image
In fur and evening and summer and spring
Of her who was different in each.

Pull down the blind and lie on the bed
And clasp the hour in the glass of one room
Against your mouth like a crystal doom.
Take up the book and stare at the letters
Hieroglyphs on sand and as meaningless –
Here birds crossed once and a foot once trod
In a mist where sight and sound are blurred.

The story of others who made their mistakes
And of one whose happiness pierced like a star
Eludes and evades between sentences
And the letters break into eyes which read
The story life writes now in your head
As though the characters sought for some clue

To their being transcendently living and dead
In your history, worse than theirs, but true.

Set in the mind of their poet, they compare
Their tragic sublime with your tawdry despair
And they have fingers which accuse
You of the double way of shame.
At first you did not love enough
And afterwards you loved too much
And you lacked the confidence to choose
And you have only yourself to blame.

Air Raid Across the Bay
at Plymouth

1

Above the whispering sea
And waiting rocks of black coast,
Across the bay, the searchlight beams
Swing and swing back across the sky.

Their ends fuse in a cone of light
Held for a bright instant up
Until they break away again
Smashing that image like a cup.

2

Delicate aluminium girders
Project phantom aerial masts
Swaying crane and derrick
Above the seas' just lifting deck.

3

Triangles, parallels, parallelograms,
Experiment with hypotheses
On the blackboard sky,
Seeking that X
Where the enemy is met.
Two beams cross
To chalk his cross.

4

A sound, sounding ragged, unseen
Is chased by two swords of light.

A thud. An instant when the whole night gleams.
Gold sequins shake out of a black-silk screen.

5

Jacob ladders slant
Up to the god of war
Who, from his heaven-high car,
Unloads upon a star
A destroying star.

Round the coast, the waves
Chuckle between rocks.
In the fields the corn
Sways, with metallic clicks.
Man hammers nails in Man,
High on his crucifix.

Memento

Remember the blackness of that flesh
Tarring the bones with a thin varnish
Belsen Theresenstadt Buchenwald where
Faces were a clenched despair
Knocking at the bird-song-fretted air.

Their eyes sunk jellied in their holes
Were held up to the sun like begging bowls
Their hands like rakes with finger-nails of rust
Scratched for a little kindness from the dust.
To many, in its beak, no dove brought answer.

Elegy for Margaret

I

Darling of our hearts, drowning
In the thick night of ultimate sea
Which (indeed) surrounds us all, but where we
Are crammed islands of flesh, wide
With a few harvesting years, disowning
The bitter black severing tide;

Here in this room you are outside this room,
Here in this body your eyes drift away,
While the invisible vultures feed on
Your life, and those who read the doom
Of the ill-boding omens say
Name of a disease which, like a villain,

Seizes on the pastures of your flesh,
Then gives you back some acres, soon again
To set you on that rack of pain
Where the skeleton cuts through you like a knife,
And the weak eyes flinch with their hoping light
Which, where we wait, blinds our still hoping sight.

Until hope signs us to despair – what lives
Seems what most kills – what holds back fate
Seems itself fated – and the eyes that smile
Mirror the mocking illness that contrives
Moving away some miles
To ricochet at one appointed date.

Least of our world, yet you are most this world
Today, when those who are well are those who hide

In dreams painted by unfulfilled desire
From hatred triumphing outside:
And where the brave, who live and love, are hurled
Through waters of a flood shot through with fire;

Where sailors' eyes rolling on floors of seas
Hold in their luminous darkening irises
The memory of some lost still dancing girl,
The possible attainable happy peace
Of statued Europe with its pastures fertile,
Dying, like a girl, of a doomed, hidden disease.

So, to be honest, I must wear your death
Next to my heart, where others wear their love.
Indeed it is my love, my link with life
My word of life being knowledge of such death.
My dying words because of you can live,
Crowned with your death, this life upon my breath.

2

From a tree choked by ivy, rotted
By kidney-shaped fungus on the bark,
Out of a topmost branch,
A spray of leaves is seen
That shoots against the ice-cold sky its mark.
The dying tree still has the strength to launch
The drained life of the sap
Into that upward arrowing glance
Above the strangling cords of evergreen.

So with you, Margaret,
Where you are lying,
The tree-trunk of your limbs choked back
By what destroys you – yet

Above the sad grey flesh
What smile surmounts your dying
On the peak of your gaze!

How tediously time kills
While the difficult breath
Asserts one usual, laughing word
Above this languor of death.
Like a water-clock it fills
The hollow well of bones
Drop by drop with dying –
Yet all that life we knew,
The eyes hold still.

How, when you have died,
Shall we remember to forget,
And with knives to separate
This life from this death:
Since, Margaret, there is never a night,
But the beflagged pride of your youth
In all its joy, does not float
Upon my sleep, as on a boat.

3

Poor girl, inhabitant of a stark land,
Where death covers your gaze,
As though the full moon might
Cast over the midsummer blaze
Its bright and dead white pall of night.

Poor child, you wear your summer dress,
And black shoes striped with gold
As today its variegated cover
Of feathery grass and spangling flowers

Delineating colour over
Shadows within which bells are tolled.

I look into your sunk eyes,
Shafts of wells to both our hearts
Which cannot take part in the lies
Of acting these gay parts.
Under our lips, our minds
Become one with the weeping
Of that mortality
Which through sleep is unsleeping.

Of what use is my weeping?
It does not carry a surgeon's knife
To cut the wrongly-multiplying cells
At the root of your life.
All it can prove
Is that extremes of love
Reach the Arctic Pole of the white bone
Where panic fills the night in which we are
    alone.

Yet my grief for you is myself, a dream,
Tomorrow's light will sweep away.
It does not wake day after day
To the same facts that are and do not seem:
The changeless changing facts around your bed,
Poverty-stricken hopeless ugliness
Of the fact that you will soon be dead.

4

i

Already you are beginning to become
Fallen tree-trunk with sun-sculptured limbs

In a perspective of dead branches and dry bones
Encircled by encroaching monumental stones.

ii

Those that begin to cease to be your eyes
Are flowers whose petals fade and honey dries
Crowded over with end-of-summer butterflies.
Wings gather to night's thickening memories.
Peacock, Red Admiral, Fritillaries,
Fly to your eyes and fly up from our gaze.

iii

Against the wall, you are already partly ghost
Whispering scratching existence almost lost
To our vulgar blatant life that eats through rooms
Our vulgar blatant life like heaped-up transient blooms.

iv

You are so quiet; your hand on the sheet seems a mouse
Yet when we turn away, the flails
That pound and beat you down with ceaseless pulse
Shake like steam hammers through the house.

v

Evening brings the opening of the windows.
Now your last sunset throws
Shadows from the roots of trees
And thrusting hounds unleashes.
In the sky fades the cinder of a rose.
Eumenides strain forwards.
The pack of night stretches towards us.

5

The final act of love
Is not of dear and dear
Blue-bird-shell eye pink-sea-shell ear
Dove twining neck with dove;

Oh no, it is the world-storm fruit
Sperm of tangling distress,
Mouth raging in the wilderness,
Fingernail tearing at dry root.

The deprived, fanatic lover
Naked in the desert
Of all except his heart
In his abandon must cover

With wild lips and torn hands,
With blanket made from his own hair,
With comfort made from his despair
The sexless corpse laid in the sands.

He pursues that narrow path
Where the sunk eye leads to the skull
And the skull into spaces, full
Of lilies, and death.

Dazed, he finds himself among
Saints, who slept with hideous sins,
Whose tongues take root on ruins,
And their language fills his tongue:

'How far we travelled, sweetheart,
Since that day when first we chose

Each other as each other's rose
And put all other worlds apart.

'Now we assume this coarseness
Of loved and loving bone
Where all are all and all alone
And to love means to bless
Everything and everyone.'

6

(To J.H.S.)

Dearest and nearest brother,
No word can turn to day
The freezing night of silence
Where all your dawns delay
Watching flesh of your Margaret
Wither in sickness away.

Yet those we lose, we learn
With singleness to love:
Regret stronger than passion holds
Her the times remove:
All those past doubts of life, her death
One happiness does prove.

Better in death to know
The happiness we lose
Than die in life in meaningless
Misery of those
Who lie beside chosen
Companions they never chose.

Orpheus, maker of music,
Clasped his pale bride
Upon that terrible river
Of those who have died;
Then of his poems the uttermost
Laurel sprang from his side.

When your red eyes follow
Her body dazed and hurt
Under the torrid mirage
Of delirious desert,
Her breasts break with white lilies,
Her eyes with Margaret.

I bring no consolation
Of the weeping shower
Whose final dropping jewel deletes
All grief in the sun's power:
You must watch the signs grow worse
Day after day, hour after hour.

Yet to accept the worst
Is finally to revive
When we are equal with the force
Of that with which we strive
And having almost lost, at last
Are glad to be alive.

As she will live who, candle-lit
Floats upon her final breath
The ceiling of the frosty night
And her high room beneath,
Wearing not like destruction, but
Like a white dress, her death.

One

Here then
She lies
Her hair a scroll along
The grooved warm nape
Her lips half-meeting on a smile
Breath almost unbreathing
O life
A word this word my love upon the white
Linen
As though I wrote her name out on this page

My concentra-
tion on her quietness
Intensifies light from this lamp
That throws its halo upward on the ceiling

Here we
Are one
Here where my waking walks upon her sleep
One within one
And darkly meeting in the hidden child.

Ice

To M —

She came in from the snowing air
Where icicle-hung architecture
Strung white fleece round the Baroque square.
I saw her face freeze in her fur,
Then my lips ran to her with fire
From the chimney corner of the room,
Where I had waited in my chair.
I kissed their heat against her skin
And watched the red make the white bloom,
While, at my care, her smiling eyes
Shone with the brilliance of the ice
Outside, whose dazzling they brought in.
  That day, until this, I forgot.
How is it now I so remember
Who, when she came indoors, saw not
The passion of her white December?

The Trance

Sometimes, apart in sleep, by chance,
You fall out of my arms, alone,
Into the chaos of your separate trance.
My eyes gaze through your forehead, through the bone,
And see where in your sleep distress has torn
Its violent path, which on your lips is shown
And on your hands and in your dream forlorn.

Restless, you turn to me, and press
Those timid words against my ear
Which thunder at my heart like stones.
'Mercy,' you plead, Then 'Who can bless?'
You ask. 'I am pursued by Time,' you moan.
I watch that precipice of fear
You tread, naked in naked distress.

To that deep care we are committed
Beneath the wildness of our flesh
And shuddering horror of our dream,
Where unmasked agony is permitted.
Our bodies, stripped of clothes that seem,
And our souls, stripped of beauty's mesh,
Meet their true selves, their charms outwitted.

This pure trance is the oracle
That speaks no language but the heart,
Our angel with our devil meets
In the atrocious dark nor do they part
But each each forgives and greets,
And their mutual terrors heal
Within our married miracle.

O

O thou O
Of round earth of round heaven,
Unfold thy wings,
Then beyond blue
Pass, beyond light
Pass, into space, out of sight

Beyond sight
O, into pure sound
Where one trumpet
Sustains the final note,
Omega, sound
Of pure silence

Beyond silence
O at the throne of God
Beyond flesh pass
Beyond form to idea
O metamorphosis
Beyond God to godlessness.

Return now
To thyself, O,
Bite thy own tail
Hoop thy own hoop

Loop thy own loop
Become that hole
Through which the eye leaps
Beyond the page, O
Word of beginning with
Nothing the end.

To My Daughter

Bright clasp of her whole hand around my finger,
My daughter, as we walk together now.
All my life I'll feel a ring invisibly
Circle this bone with shining: when she is grown
Far from today as her eyes are far already.

Nocturne

Their six-weeks-old daughter lies
In her cot, crying out the night. Their hearts
Are sprung like armies, waiting
To cross the gap to where her loneliness
Lies infinite between them. This child's cry
Sends rays of a star's pain through endless dark;
And the sole purpose of their loving
Is to disprove her demonstration
Of all love's aidlessness. Words unspoken
Out of her mouth unsaying, prove unhappiness
Pure as innocence, virgin of tragedy,
Unknowing reason. Star on star of pain
Surround her cry to make a constellation
Where human tears of victims are the same
As griefs of the unconscious animals.

Listening, the parents know this primal cry
Out of the gates of life, hollows such emptiness,
It proves that all men's aims should be, all times,
To fill the gap of pain with consolation
Poured from the mountain-sided adult lives
Whose minds like peaks attain to heights of snow:
The snow should stoop to wash away such grief.
Unceasing love should lave the feet of victims.

Yet, when they lift their heads out of such truths,
Today mocks at their prayers. To think this even
Suffices to remind them of far worse
Man-made man-destroying ills which threaten
While they try to lull a child. For she
Who cries for milk, for rocking, and a shawl,
Is also subject to the rage of causes

Dividing peoples. Even at this moment
Eyes might fly between them and the moon,
And a hand touch a lever to let fall
That which would make the street of begging roofs
Pulverize and creep skywards in a tower:
Down would fall baby, cradle, and them all.

That which sent out the pilot to destroy them
Was the same will as that with which they send
An enemy to kill their enemy. Even in this love
Running in shoals on each side of her bed,
Is fear, and hate. If they shift their glances
From her who weeps, their eyes meet other eyes
Willed with death, also theirs. All would destroy
New-born, innocent streets. Necessity,
With abstract head and searing feet, men's god
Unseeing the poor amulets of flesh,
Unhearing the minutiae of prayer.

Parents like mountains watching above their child,
Envallied here beneath them, also hold
Upon their frozen heights, the will that sends
Destruction into centres of the stones
Which concentrated locked centennial stillness
For human generations to indwell.

Hearing their daughter's cry which is the speech
Of indistinguishable primal life,
They know the dark is filled with means which are
Men's plots to murder children. They know too
No cause is just unless it guards the innocent
As sacred trust: no truth but that
Which reckons this child's tears an argument.

If It Were Not

If it were not for that
Lean executioner, who stands
Ever beyond a door
With axe raised in both hands –

All my days here would be
One day – the same – the drops
Of light edgeless in light
That no circumference stops.

Mountain, star or flower
Single with my seeing
Would – gone from sight – draw back again
Each to its separate being

Nor would I hoard against
The obliterating desert
Their crystals of the petalled snow
Glittering on the heart.

My hand would never stir
To follow into stone
Hair the wind outlines on sky
A moment, and then gone.

What gives edge to remembering
Is death. It's that shows, curled
Within each falling moment
An Antony, a world.

She came into the garden
And walking through deep grass, held up

Our child who, smiling down at her,
Clung to her throat, a cup.

Clocks notch such instances
On time: no time to keep
Beyond the eye's delight
The loss that makes it weep.

I chisel memories
Within a shadowy room
Transmuting gleams of light to ships
Launched into a tomb.

What Love Poems Say

In spite of this
Enormity of space
Total distance total dark between
Lights all fire all ice
Adverse to all of life –

Nevertheless, I wake
This morning to this luck, that you
On a second of a clock
Into a measured space, this room,
Come, as though
Spiralling down a staircase of
Immeasurable light-years –
Here and now made flesh
With greeting in your eyes,
Lips smiling, willing to respond,
Hand extended.

It is as though I were
In all the universe the centre
Of a circumference
Surrounding us with lights
That have eyes watchful, benevolent –
Looked on us and concentrated
Their omnipresence in one instance –
You, come with a word.

Sleepless

Awake alone in the house
I heard a voice
Ambiguous
With nothing nice.

Perhaps knocking windows?
A board loose in the floor?
A gap where a draught blows
Under the door?

Repairs needed? Bills?
Is it owls hooting – Pay! –
Or it might be the walls
Crumbling away

Reminding – 'You too
Disintegrate
With the plaster – but you
At a faster rate.'

Or it might be that friend once
I shut outside
– Sink or swim – well, he sank –
In my sleep cried

'Let me in! Let me in!'
Tapping at the pane –
Him I imagine –
Twenty years in the rain.

STEPHEN SPENDER

Voice from a Skull

Futami-ga-ura, Ise-Shima

(*for Peter Watson*)

1

Here, where the Pacific seems a pond,
Winds like pocket knives have carved out islands
To netsuke ...
                    Pekingese
With rampant ruffs and fanned-out claws
Scratch at coiff'd waves; a pirate junk
Lobs cones from conifers
                              (its mast
That solitary pine trunk staved
With two bone boughs);
                              porcupine;
Tortoise; dragon; cormorant.

2

                    Our boat throbs on
Through sea and sky, the seamless bowl
Of solid light, in which pearl fishers dive.
It thrusts through scarcely lifting waves:
A stretching and unstretching surface.
Oars of fisher boats are delicate
As crochet needles.

3

                    We land
Where a path skirts the coast. Twined ropes
Are slung between twin boulders to lasso

At dawn the sun, risen for pilgrims.
Following the path I reach a park
With cliffs hewn into caves embossed
With hieroglyphs ...

               In one cave
A hermit sits. He scrapes a tune upon
One hair outstretched of his white beard,
His bow's his bone-brown arm.

4

Suddenly I hear your voice –
Inside my skull your voice – in those
Gay mocking tones I knew:

                  'You were
Once my companion on a journey
The far side of the world, the Alps,
Rock-leaded windows of Europe.
You saw their sky and grass upon my eyes
Who am dragged under soil in a net
That tangles smile and eye-balls with
Their visions rainbowed still ...

                    But you
Lacking my eyes through which you looked,
Turn like a shadow round the sunlit dial.'

Fifteen Line Sonnet in Four Parts

1

When we talk, I imagine silence
Beyond the intervalling words: a space
Empty of all but ourselves there, face to face,
Away from others, alone in the intense
Light or dark, it would not matter which.

2

But where a room envelopes us, one heart,
Our bodies locked together prove apart
Unless we change them back again to speech.

3

Close to here, looking at you, I see
Beyond your eyes looking back, that second you
Of whom the outward semblance is but image –
The inmost being where the name springs true.

4

Today, left only with a name, I rage,
Willing these lines, as though a word could be
Flesh, on the blank unanswering page.

V.W., 1941

That woman who, entering a room,
Stood looking round at all, with rays
Of her wild eyes, till people there
– And books, pictures, furniture –
Became transformed within her gaze
To rocks, fish, wrecks, Armada treasure,
Gold lit green on the sea floor –

Filled her dress with heavy stones
Then lay down in a shallow brook
Where a wave like casing glass
Curves over her shattered face,
And clothes, torn pages of her book,
Mad mind as cold and silent as the stones.

On the Photograph of a Friend, Dead

Dead friend, the snapshot proves there was an instant
That with a place – leaf-dazzling garden – crossed
When – mirror of midday – you sent
Shadows and light from your real flesh into
The sensitive dark instrument

That took your image for its opposite
And, in a black cell, stood you on your head.
On the film, when I developed it,
Black showed white where you had shadows, white
Black, where, looking up, your eyes were sunlit.

To me, under my hand, in the dark room,
Laid in a bath of chemicals, your ghost
Emerged gelatinously from that tomb;
Looking glass, soot-faced, values all reversed,
Shadows brilliant and the lights all gloom.

Reverse of that reverse, your photograph
Now positively scans me with
Your quizzical ironic sad half-laugh:
The gaze oblique under sun-sculptured lids
Endlessly asks me 'Is this all we have?'

Lost Days

(For John Lehmann)

Then, when an hour was twenty hours, he lay
Drowned under grass. He watched the carrier ant
With mandibles as trolley, push in front
Wax-yellow specks across the parched cracked clay.

A tall sun made the stems down there transparent.
Moving, he saw the speedwell's sky blue eye
Start up next to his own, a chink of sky
Stamped deep through the tarpaulin of a tent.

He pressed his mouth against the rooted ground.
Held in his arms, he felt the earth spin round.

Matter of Identity

Who he was, remained an open question
He asked himself, looking at all those others –
Successes, roaring down the street –

Explorer, politician, bemedalled
General, teacher – any of these
He might have been. But he was none.

Impossible, though, to avoid the conclusion
That he had certain attributes: for instance,
Parents, birthday, sex. Calendars

Each year the same day totted up his age.
Also he was a husband and had children
And fitted in an office, measure of his desk.

Yet he never felt quite certain
Even of certainties: discerned a gap
(Like that between two letters) between statistics

(These he was always writing out on forms)
And his real self. Sometimes he wondered
Whether he had ever been born, or had died ...

(A blank space dreaming of its asterisks)

　　　*　　　　*　　　　*

Sometimes he had the sensation
Of being in a library and reading a history

And coming to a chapter left unwritten
That blazed with nothing ... nothing except him.
– Nothing but his great name and his great deeds.

Moon

Moon, I don't believe in you!
Yet now I almost do
Seeing you (above those rectangles
Of windows – triangles
Of roofs – squares of squares –
And through those scimitars
Of silhouetted leaves)
Describe your lucid circle,
Buoyant disk exalting
A map that mocks our earth.

The Chalk Blue Butterfly

The Chalk Blue (clinging to
A harebell stem, where it loops
Its curving wirefine neck
From which there hangs the flowerbell
Shaken by the wind that shakes
Too, the butterfly)
Opens now, now shuts, its wings,
Opening, shutting, on a hinge
Sprung at touch of sun or shadow.
     Open, the sunned wings mirror
Minute, double, all the sky.
     Shut, the ghostly underwing
Is cloud-opaque, bordered by
Copper spots embossed
With a goblin hammering.

     I look and look, as though my eyes
Could hold the Chalk Blue in a vice,
Waiting for some other witness –
That child's blue gaze, miraculous.
But today I am alone.

Boy Cat Canary

Our whistling son called his canary Hector.
'Why?' I asked. 'Because I had always about me
More of Hector with his glittering helmet than
Achilles with his triple-thewed shield.' He let Hector
Out of his cage, fly up to the ceiling, perch on his chair, hop
Onto his table where the sword lay bright among books
While he sat in his yellow jersey doing his homework.
Once, hearing a shout, I entered his room, saw what carnage:
The Siamese cat had worked his tigerish scene.
Hector lay on the floor of his door-open cage
Wings still fluttering, flattened against the sand.
Parallel, horizontal on his rug, the boy lay
Mouth biting against it, fists drumming the boards.
'Tomorrow let him forget,' I prayed, 'let him not see
What I see in this room of miniature *Iliad* –
The golden whistling howled down by the dark.'

To Become a Dumb Thing

Sunset.
At the harbour mouth headlands
cross axe heads of transparent agate.
Boats stab needles of lights into the pleating water.
Fishermen stand or sit, on quayside, in boats, mending
   nets.
One, without a word, gets up, goes over to another,
   helps him, goes back.

*

We sit at our café table by the sea.
Talk Paris New York London – places
we shall/shan't visit.
The temples! The bull ring! The blood!
Red hot corpses embers shed in the Ganges!
Gossip! Friends! Enemies!
Playing over old scenes on a worn reel.

*

Six fishermen wade out, clamber into a boat. One
   advances to the end of a jetty to which several boats,
   with men and women in them, are tied. He pisses into
   the sea.

*

Their life is a life of things. Their thoughts are
   things. They touch things. The fish nudges against the
   hook. The hook pricks the gullet. The line tugs against
   the horned hand. The nets weigh moon-glittering
   scales.

*

They are skittles in a stone alley. At day's end the sun,
    a raging ball, topples them over one by one. Falling
    into beds. Flailing arms. Into one another's arms.
    Drunk.

*

To be them would mean throwing aside Christian's
    burden when he forsook wife and children to ...
unwind a coil ...
crawling on all fours ...
begging life from beggars ...
to become a dumb thing ...